"Jesus's and Francis's starting point was not sin, but suffering—the suffering of the world and even the suffering of God. This creates a very different perspective on the Christian gospel, and I think you will find it here! In this book, Dan Horan makes the sublime simple and beautiful, which is surely the Franciscan way."

—Richard Rohr, O.F.M.
Center for Action and Contemplation

This beautiful new book by one of my favorite young spiritual writers offers an invitation to meditate on God's great love for us, on Christ's sacrifice and on the human condition. Dan Horan's insights are for anyone who has ever grieved, lost or sought hope. In other words, it is a book for everyone.

—James Martin, S.J.
author, *The Jesuit Guide to (Almost) Everything*

Beautiful, fresh reflections on Jesus's dying words in the spirit of Francis of Assisi. The insights lead straight into ways of discipleship, empowering love of God and our neighbor in this contemporary world.

—Elizabeth Johnson, C.S.J.
distinguished professor of theology, Fordham University

Daniel Horan's passion to follow the advice of St. Francis of Assisi—"Preach the Gospel at all times; when necessary use words"—comes through clearly in these wise reflections at the foot of the cross. Highly recommended as a resource for all who seek to discover the meaning of the call to love in the face of suffering.

—Mary Catherine Hilkert, O.P.
professor of theology, University of Notre Dame

Through his moving reflections on Jesus's last words, Fr. Dan Horan demonstrates how, in our own everyday lives, God is always inviting us to open our hearts to that love. Like Jesus, we are asked to surrender our need for control and security by daring to accompany those marginalized persons who themselves continue to be crucified today. If we venture such solidarity with the outcasts of our world, we will paradoxically discover why the Gospel is indeed "Good News."

—Roberto S. Goizueta
Margaret O'Brien Flatley Professor of Catholic Theology,
Boston College

The lifeblood of these deeply Franciscan meditations is the memory of a God who is "head over heels in love with humanity," and who identifies radically with suffering creation. Dan Horan writes with the steady hand of a scholar and the trembling heart of a follower of Jesus. I will never again hear Jesus's words "I thirst" without also hearing the cries of those hidden millions today dying from lack of water. Dan helps us wrestle, as every new generation must, with the terrible beauty and scandal of the cross.

—Chris Pramuk
associate professor of theology, Xavier University

The
Last Words
of
Jesus

A Meditation on
Love and Suffering

Daniel P. Horan, O.F.M.

Franciscan
MEDIA
Cincinnati, Ohio

Adapted from reflections originally delivered at St. Francis of Assisi Church, New York, NY, April 22, 2011. Scripture citations are taken from the *New Revised Standard Version Bible*, copyright ©1989 by the Division of Christian Education of the National Council of Churches of Christ in the United States of America. Excerpts are taken from *Francis of Assisi: Early Documents*, volumes 1, 2, and 3, edited by Regis J. Armstrong, J.A. Wayne Hellmann, and William J. Short copyright ©1999–2001 The New City Press. Used by permission. Cited throughout as *FAED* followed by volume and page number.

Cover and book design by Mark Sullivan
Cover image ©Veer | Num_skyman

LIBRARY OF CONGRESS CATALOGING-IN-PUBLICATION DATA
Horan, Daniel P.
The last words of Jesus : a meditation on love and suffering / Daniel P. Horan, O.F.M.
pages cm
Includes bibliographical references and index.
ISBN 978-1-61636-409-0 (alk. paper)
1. Jesus Christ—Seven last words—Meditations. I. Title.
BT457.H67 2013
232.96'35—dc23
2013037597

ISBN 978-1-61636-409-0

Published by Franciscan Media
28 W. Liberty St.
Cincinnati, OH 45202
www.FranciscanMedia.org
www.AmericanCatholic.org

Printed in the United States of America.
Printed on acid-free paper.
14 15 16 17 18 5 4 3 2 1

CONTENTS

v

To David Golemboski—
a friend who continually inspires me
to be a better Christian
by his commitment to social justice
in our world.

ACKNOWLEDGMENTS

As the subtitle of this brief book might suggest, writing about love and suffering is no easy task. It is especially challenging when trying to grapple with the Good Friday events that represent one of the significant cornerstones of our Christian faith, while seeking to understand better the meaning of these events for our own time. The reflections contained here are the product of several opportunities I had to share my thoughts on the perennially meditative last words of Christ with a number of gracious congregations and groups.

I wish to thank Fr. Timothy Shreenan, O.F.M., my brother friars, and the staff of St. Francis of Assisi Church on Thirty-First Street in New York City for the humbling invitation to deliver the annual afternoon Good Friday reflections on the Seven Last Words in 2011. Thanks, also, to Sr. Ilia Delio, O.S.F.; Sr. Lisa Drover, O.S.F.; and the Franciscan Sisters of Washington, D.C., for the invitation to give their 2012 community Lenten retreat on this theme. I also shared some of this material at St. Francis of Assisi Church in Triangle, Virginia, when Fr. Kevin Downey, O.F.M., and the other friars there asked me to preach during the Good Friday liturgy in 2012.

Thanks go to my friend, fellow St. Bonaventure University alum and all-star editor Lisa Biedenbach for the earliest suggestion that these reflections should be developed into a book. I am grateful for her keen editorial sense for what makes a good project and the encouragement to write a text that would appeal to a broader population. Also, I am grateful for the continued encouragement and guidance of Mary Carol Kendzia, my editor and the product development director at Franciscan Media.

I owe a special note of gratitude to my brother friar Fr. John Ullrich, O.F.M., who generously offered to share his pastoral gift for leading parish discussion groups by writing the reflection questions found at the end of each chapter. John is a wonderfully generous brother with whom I have had the privilege of living in community, and whose pastoral experience and insight have helped shape my own ministry in many positive ways. May his reflection questions help this book come alive for you in reflection and through discussion.

I have been blessed throughout my life to have a number of generous, kind, intelligent, inspiring, challenging, and humorous friends. Among those I am honored to call my friends, David Golemboski and his wife, Brianna, have been all of these things above and I am grateful for their continued friendship, love, and support. David is someone whose entire young adult and adult life has been dedicated to Catholic social teaching and the work of social justice in our world. Over the years he has played a significant role in organizations like JustFaith Ministries and Witness

ACKNOWLEDGMENTS

For Peace, and was the 2007 recipient of the Cardinal Bernardin New Leadership Award from the United States Conference of Catholic Bishops for his work in educating young people about social justice. In gratitude for his friendship and in appreciation for his continued social justice work, I dedicate this book to my good friend David.

The origin of this book can be traced back to the Eastern Shore of Maryland during the first week of January 2011. All of the Franciscan friars of Holy Name Province (based in New York City) were assembled at large conference center during the off-season in order to have what is called a chapter. In religious life a *chapter* is the term used to describe the meeting that occurs every three years when all the friars who are able get together to take care of business matters, enjoy each other's company (think of a big, Franciscan family reunion), and discuss the future of the community for the following three years. January 2011 happened to be the time during which this big event was scheduled to take place.

In the hallway outside the big conference-style meeting room, while the friars chatted with one another, stretched their legs, and had some coffee, Fr. Timothy Shreenan, O.F.M., a friar stationed at the mother church of our Franciscan province, St. Francis of Assisi Parish on Thirty-First Street in New York City, approached me with an invitation. He said that every Holy Week the friars of this internationally known Church would invite a guest preacher to come to Manhattan and offer a series of reflections on the Seven Last Words of Christ on the afternoon of Good Friday. Tim said that he would like me to consider being the 2011 preacher.

Humbling as such an invitation was, my first reaction was that I was too young and too inexperienced—surely there are more seasoned friars and other preachers that would be a more natural selection. Tim's response was that it was in part for those very same reasons about which I felt unprepared for the task, that the friars were interested in having me offer these reflections. He said that my writing, particularly the then-new blog I wrote, www. DatingGod.org, had caught the attention of many who believed that my take on spirituality, theology, and Scripture might be just what the large and faithful crowd that gathered every Good Friday in midtown Manhattan needed to hear on the day the Christian community throughout the world commemorated the death of the Lord. He said that I should take a few days to think about it and get back to him with an answer by the end of the week.

That night I Googled "The Seven Last Words of Christ." Yes, that's right; while I had heard of this tradition I had never actually *attended* such a service. For several hours I read a number of web pages about the tradition of preaching on the Seven Last Words of Christ, learned a lot about Haydn's famous orchestration by that name, and pondered the seven lines that came from the different Gospel accounts. While this was something new to me, I realized that perhaps my brother Franciscans saw something in me that I would not have seen in myself. That realization, combined with my newfound interest in these seven phrases from the cross, led me the next day to tell Tim that I would be honored to come to New York City to preach on Good Friday.

When I pressed for more information about what might be expected, I got two responses. First, part of the draw of the St. Francis of Assisi Parish's service on the Seven Last Words was precisely the variety of preachers over the course of many years. Each person invited has come and offered a unique take on perhaps the most reflected on lines from the passion narratives. I would have a lot of freedom in how I presented my reflections on these scriptural excerpts from Christ on the cross.

Second, I was told not to be too brief in my reflections. Now I can assure you that this was the first time—and very likely the last time—that anyone had ever advised me to be sure that my homily was (make that, homil*ies* were) not too *short*. I was told that people travel very long distances each year to hear, reflect, and pray, and that they would not be in a rush to go anywhere. In fact, those in attendance may actually be disappointed if I erred on the side of brevity. Talk about counterintuitive advice!

Those were my guiding parameters. For my own part, I took the opportunity to meditate on and reflect upon these seven lines (words) throughout Lent. This would be my Lenten practice that year, allowing the last words of Christ to speak to my heart in whatever ways the Spirit would inspire. In the ordinary activities of showering in the morning, running in the afternoon, walking across campus on the way to teach my classes, sitting quietly in the Friary chapel for prayer, wherever I was, these lines were like a whisper in the background of my forty-day journey.

I was surprised at what surfaced.

Along the way I had made sure to read several scriptural commentaries by noted scholars so that I could feel as though I really understood what the words of Christ meant in context. That was the easy part. It was the way in which those words spoke to me in our own day, in this world some two millennia after they were first spoken, that was the transformative experience.

Traditionally, preachers tasked with reflecting on these words have zeroed in on perennial themes like forgiveness, Mary as our mother, reconciliation, and trust, to name a few. While these sorts of foci are valuable and edifying in their own right, they were not what I felt called to examine. Instead, it was the subthemes and overlooked words that spoke to my heart. The way in which these words and themes addressed me was not always in the key of comfort and rest, but oftentimes in the unsettling power that the Gospel can have as the words of Christ tug on the hearts of believers.

There is a challenge and an invitation latent in the last words of Christ, much as there is in all of his words found in the Gospel. I began to realize that as these words challenged me to be a better Christian, to examine how it is that I do or do not follow the model of Jesus Christ, these two were supposed to be words to challenge all believers. This would be my mission. This is what I would do.

Over the course of several days in a cabin in the Adirondack Mountains, something of a retreat and renewal site for the Franciscan friars who minister at Siena College near Albany, New York, I sat down to write down the reflections that had come into clearer and clearer relief over the course of my Lenten journey. While I had minimal external guidance on how to formulate and present these reflections, I provided myself with three principles that would shape my approach.

First, I would always offer a scripturally sound reflection. A danger in any form of preaching is to simply apply one's own reading to the text without at least a grounding appreciation for the meaning, history, and context of the passage. I was committed to offering a fresh take on the Seven Last Words; that was, of course, one of the reasons I was invited to do this, and I had no desire to simply reiterate the centuries-old tropes that had become so closely associated with each of these words, something I felt produced a caricature of Jesus's last comments. Where I would offer something that might sound novel, I was committed to at least acknowledging how the given passage had been classically interpreted.

Second, I would offer these reflections in a consciously Franciscan tenor. Frankly, I feel as though I could not have done otherwise. The spiritual, theological, and philosophical tradition of the Franciscan community has been the most formative feature of my understanding of Christian discipleship. For those who might appreciate a music metaphor, I felt as though one of the ways these reflections would be different from others was that I would intentionally change the key of the tune. The song remained the same, but if the song was normally heard in the traditional key of C-major I was going to shift the music to the Franciscan key of B-flat. The musical themes of the Christian tradition and the scriptural harmonic landmarks would be the same, but playing the score in a new key could allow for even the most seasoned hearer of the word to listen to the nuances of the Spirit in a way previously unexpected. A key change doesn't change the song, but changes the way we hear it.

Finally, I was committed to not shying away from the strong themes of social justice present in the words from the cross. Sticking with the music imagery, the problem with knowing a song so well is that we forget to listen to it and instead rely on our own memory of what it sounds like. I'm not sure about you, but I can glaze over and zone out if I begin to hear something I have heard many times before.

One of the concerns that I have as a young minister and teacher is that the Gospels have become too domesticated. Part of the struggle is cultural and contextual: Our worlds are just not rocked by Jesus's one-time scandalous table fellowship or stories about Jews and Samaritans anymore. The edge has been taken off of what is, at times, a subversive and painfully challenging message that those who follow Christ dare to call the "Good News"! Forgiving the unforgivable, embracing the unlovable, healing the broken, clothing the naked, loving the enemy—these are not fairy tales simply to be admired nor are they cute allegories to be placed on a shelf, dusted occasionally, and viewed from afar.

The good news we call Gospel is the good news according to God, which, lest we ignore St. Paul, is foolish to the wise, a stumbling block to some, and despised by the worldly. I am convinced, especially after spending some intense time in reflecting on Jesus's final earthly words to us as he suffered and died, that if there was ever a collection of New Testament passages that should challenge us to live more for others as God has lived for us, it is the Seven Last Words of Christ. His parting words from this life should be the founding words of my life.

What follows, then, is an extended version of what I first presented in the sanctuary of that beautiful church in Manhattan (perhaps its interior is most famously recalled from the live broadcast of the Mass of Christian Burial for my brother in Franciscan life, Fr. Mychal Judge, O.F.M., chaplain to the New York City Fire Department and the first registered death of the victims of the 9/11 terrorist attacks).

In a world that remains irrevocably shaped by the suffering of the human condition, the misunderstanding between groups and cultures symbolized by the horrific events of September 11, we need to hear Christ's words anew. Not just any words, but those uttered by one who also suffered and by one who also died. Indeed these are not just any words, but the words of a God who so loved the world that Word became one like us. Our invitation, our challenge today, is to become like him, to live up to the name that we bear when we call ourselves Christians.

Daniel P. Horan, O.F.M.
Solemnity of St. Bonaventure
July 15, 2012

PASSION, CONTROL, AND A FRANCISCAN PERSPECTIVE ON THE CROSS OF CHRIST

The cross is perhaps the greatest paradox in the history of salvation. On the one hand, it is the greatest symbol of love. From Jesus's embrace of what stood before him in the garden of Gethsemane to his final moments on the cross, we have embodied the self-sacrificing love about which Jesus preached during his ministry ("No one has greater love than this, to lay down one's life for one's friends"—John 15:13) and, as we hear in St. Paul's words about Christ being "the image of the invisible God" (Colossians 1:15), we have a glimpse at the unconditional love of our Creator present in the self-offering of the crucifixion. Yet, on the other hand, the cross remains a stark symbol of suffering. What could be more painful than being nailed to a tree to die of asphyxiation and exposure to the elements after having been tortured? To speak of the cross is, by definition, to speak of suffering.

So how do we reconcile these seemingly opposed aspects of one of the most important events of our history and faith? Is there a way to understand the place of both love and suffering on the cross and in our lives? What insight might the Franciscan spiritual tradition offer us in making sense of Good Friday?

This book takes a unique look at the tradition of the Seven Last Words of Christ on Good Friday, a source of reflection and prayer that Christians have returned to time and again through the centuries. Dozens of authors, most of whom are better apt to offer their insights and reflections on these sayings of Christ than I am, have published books on Good Friday and these seven scriptural snippets that seem to capture the attention, imagination, and heart of Christians every year.

My contribution to this library of Lenten meditations is not intended to be a definitive commentary on these perennially important words from the cross, but another look, from another vantage point, from another time, so that another generation might discover the wisdom latent in just a few words and so that others might renew their outlook in rediscovering what it is the God is continually revealing to us through Scripture.

The three guiding questions raised above—dealing with the reconciliation of love and suffering, understanding the place of these two aspects of the cross and in our lives, and exploring the Franciscan contributions to our understanding of the event of the cross—are not going to be definitively answered in the subsequent chapters and pages. Instead, it is my hope that, in keeping these ever-present themes in mind, we might better be able to reflect on the way these last words speak to each of us.

Furthermore, as the former Dominican Master General Timothy Radcliffe explains so well, it is my additional hope that we might better be able to understand how Christ's words before his death on the cross not only speak *to us* from his life and reality, but also speak *for us* in our own settings, locations, and history.[1] The power of what was uttered in that ultimate experience of love and suffering is not just relevant for one or for many, but for all.

PASSION: A COIN THAT HAS TWO SIDES

One of the real tragedies of our contemporary United States culture is that so few of those who were born and raised in this context are polyglots, people fluent in several languages. If you're like me, you might have studied a second language in high school or college, but you probably did not grow up speaking several languages. If you come from a family of recent immigrants, as opposed to so many other United States citizens who come from a family of earlier immigrants, you might be an exception to that presumption. Nevertheless, there is still a lack of linguistic diversity in our broader culture. Unlike the countries of the European Union, for example, which regularly cater to a whole array of languages in the public square, English has a nearly universal presence and power in our society. Those who do not speak English or speak it well may find it difficult to negotiate the complexities of modern life in certain parts of the United States.

However, what many of those who are native English speakers without substantial appreciation for another language miss in everyday life is the importance of translation, word choice, and the etymology or history of a given word's origin, development, and usage. As true as this lack of appreciation is in the social sphere, it is even truer when it comes to our Christian faith.

Christianity and its sacred Scriptures bear a multiple-millennia history that begins with the oral tradition that came to be written down as the Hebrew Scriptures (what many Christians call the Old Testament) and continues through to our present day in the modern vernacular translations of our sacred texts. Words have a history and a meaning, an origin and tradition of usage, a way of implying complex ideas and concepts that can often elude us when we only think about the way we use words in our native languages, especially if that language is modern American English.

The centrality of words and the importance of language stand at the heart of the Christian tradition. Timothy Radcliffe makes this point very clear in the introduction to his own reflection on the Seven Last Words some years ago:

> The Christian story is a drama about words and their meaning, God's words and ours. It begins with the Word through which everything came to be...our words give life or death; they create or destroy. The climax of this drama is Jesus' last words on the cross. We treasure them because here is rooted our faith that human words do indeed reach after and touch some ultimate destiny and purpose.[2]

4

Among the many words that "reach after and touch some ulti-mate destiny and purpose" is the word *passion*. Like the paradox of the cross itself, bearing both the symbols of love and suffering, the word passion bears seemingly different meanings that can appear to be in opposition to one another, but the word passion isn't really a contronym (a word that means one thing and its opposite, such as the word *cleave*, which can be used to mean splitting apart or adhering together). *Passion* is a word in that has a profound significance that touches the human experience in two very important ways.

On the one hand, passion is most commonly used today to describe the love someone has for another person, for some activity, or for some object. Here we might think of the romantic drive, energy, and dedication that a person madly in love with another person exhibits. This is captured in so much creative art and popular culture over recent centuries. Consider, for example, the opening stanza of the poem "Love" by the seventeenth-century author Samuel Taylor Coleridge:

> All thoughts, all passions, all delights,
> Whatever stirs this mortal frame,
> All are but ministers of Love,
> And feed his sacred flame.[3]

In this sense love is the implication and love is the force most closely associated with one's passion, and it is the meaning that people today are likely to associate with hearing the word *passion*. This romantic connotation first appeared in some religious writing of the fourteenth century in which the Greek word for emotion—*pathos*—was translated into the Latin word for passion. However, it didn't come to be widely used in this sense until around the sixteenth century after the first recorded use of the term to describe "sexual love or emotion" explicitly by none other than Shakespeare in *Titus Andronicus* around 1588.[4] Today the term is often used in less romantic but still in positive colloquial ways, such as when we speak about one's passion for sports, work, or a hobby. When we talk about somebody's passion, we generally mean some kind of love.

But that is not what the word originally meant. The word passion comes from the Latin word *passio*, which means "suffering" or "enduring." This implication is far less rosy and much more dark. Passion, in this sense, conveys the pain that comes with cruel and unusual punishment, enduring through the trials of great suffering, and stands in a place wholly other than the way passion has been used to describe love in popular ways. The origin of this usage also has a very Christian foundation. As far as all the linguistic and etymological research suggests, its primary meaning has always been associated with the crucifixion of Jesus Christ.

So what are we to make of this twofold meaning of the word *passion*?

Love and suffering are really two sides of the same coin that we call passion. Like passion's original meaning in reference to the crucifixion of Christ, love and suffering have a lot to do with our lives as Christian women and men in our own times and places. At first glance, love and suffering seem like incompatible experiences or emotions. When one thinks about the love of another, it is usually joy, happiness, or contentment that registers in our imagination and hearts.

A similar thing takes place when we think about suffering, for suffering tends to be the domain of those lacking love, those lacking the joy, happiness, or contentment that we associate with the other meaning of passion. But it's not quite as simple as that. Love and suffering are far more intimately linked than we might wish to acknowledge.

This hit home for me in a very clear way when my grandfather died and I, as a friar, was preparing to preach the homily for his funeral Mass. It occurred to me that all of us who gathered in that church came to the liturgy with very heavy hearts. This figurative language became very helpful in articulating the strong emotions we all experienced, to a degree that was almost physical, as if our hearts were indeed weighed down with a sense of grief and the acknowledgment of loss.

But it also occurred to me one's heart could be heavy with love as much as it could be heavy with suffering. One's heart can be so full of love that it feels as if it were going to burst at any moment. Think of someone you love with all of your heart. There are times when the love, the desire, the need to connect with another weighs on our hearts to such an extent that it too aches with an emotional and spiritual heaviness. My extended family came to the church to celebrate the funeral Mass of my grandfather, along with his surviving friends, and we did so because we cared about Les Murphy Jr. with a passion that was not just about suffering, but with a passion that was also about love.

The passion of love necessarily implies suffering. They are inextricably intertwined, whether we realize it or not, whether we like it or not. I would suggest that the at least implicit appreciation for the connection between the experiences of love and suffering among the human population has led to this theme's presence in many popular cultural venues. Take, for example, the 1976 song "Love Hurts" by the band Nazareth. While the lyrics ultimately suggest that the happiness people presume comes with love is really just a lie, there is a telling dimension to the opening description of what love does: it hurts, it scars, it wounds, it mars, and love brings with it a lot of pain. Later in the song we are again reminded of the suffering that love implies: "Love is like a flame / It burns you when it's hot." The image of fire in discussing passion is something that others have seen as helpful, particularly for its alluring and fear-inducing potential. It is for this reason that author Susan Pitchford titles a chapter "Pyrophobia: In Fear of the Flame" in her book on suffering and desire in the spiritual life.[5]

Another, rather cute, example of the acknowledgment of the suffering that comes on the heels of love can be seen in the popular 2003 British film *Love Actually*. The scene is when Daniel, a single father played by actor Liam Neeson, sits on a park bench beside his not-quite-teenage son Sam, played by actor Thomas Brodie-Sangster, and tries to find out what has been upsetting the boy lately. Daniel initially presumes it is Sam's continued grieving of his recently deceased mother. He then asks if it's bullying at school. Still without a response, the father asks his son, "Is it something worse?" At this point Sam asks his father whether or not he really wants to know what's wrong.

> **Daniel:** I really want to know.
>
> **Sam:** Even though you won't be able to do anything about it?
>
> **Daniel:** Even if that's the case, yeah.
>
> **Sam:** Okay, well...the truth is, actually...I'm in love.
>
> **Daniel:** Sorry?
>
> **Sam:** I know I should be thinking about Mum all the time, and I am, but the truth is...I'm in love, and I was before she died, and there's nothing I can do about it.
>
> **Daniel:** Aren't you a bit young to be in love?
>
> **Sam:** No.
>
> **Daniel:** Oh, okay, right...Well, I'm a little relieved.
>
> **Sam:** Why?
>
> **Daniel:** Well, because I...I thought it would be something worse.
>
> **Sam:** Worse than the total agony of being in love?
>
> **Daniel:** Um... No, you're right. Total agony.[6]

From puppy love to the most complicated of mature relationships, love in its manifold form includes its own share of suffering. As the young Sam put it so well, being in love with another is an experience so wrought with emotions, so consuming of energy, so unique in its particular manifestation, that perhaps the only way to describe the experience is as a form of agony. Total agony.

The Giving Up and the Taking Away of Control

The thing that makes love agonizing, in a way, is that it recalls the suffering that is centered on control, our desire to maintain it, and the risk of losing it in our life. Both the experience of falling in love and the experience of suffering arise from a loss of control. In the case of love, control is given up. One surrenders his or her individual control for something else, for the interdependence of relationship that, as my fellow Franciscan friar Richard Rohr has said, "makes you willing to risk everything, holding nothing back."[7]

If love is the free surrender of one's control, then suffering is the involuntary taking of that control away. Rohr likes to say that suffering is simply defined as "whenever you are not in control."[8] It's not so difficult now to see how the line between love and suffering is both thin and blurry. The significance of control, its surrender and its loss, plays an important role in our faith and is a focal point of our reflection on the experience of Jesus Christ on the cross. Rather than try to demarcate whether what Jesus is most immediately experiencing and expressing on the cross is love or suffering, we can reflect on the unity of these two experiences in the event of the crucifixion and in our own lives.

If there's one thing about which we can all agree, being crucified as a criminal and enemy of the Roman state is about as out of control as one can be. There are plenty of people who get very uncomfortable with this sort of statement, and some folks might ask: "But doesn't Jesus's full divinity mean that he was always in control? Surely, God never loses control." Yet, by definition, to love is to surrender one's self, at least in part, to the vulnerabilities of another's will. You cannot make someone love you, but you can let go of the need to control whether and how the other person responds to your love.

Because of our free will, that tremendous gift from God, we cannot be controlled into loving God back in response to the unconditional love God already has for us. As odd as it sounds, God's very love for humanity and the rest of creation resembles, in some way, our own experience of love and suffering in our human relationships. The very love that has brought us into creation, into existence, and into the possibility of loving at all provides the condition for God's surrender of control. There is perhaps no better example than the cross to highlight this truth.

The love of Jesus Christ that leads to his willing embrace of the crucified earthly destiny that appeared before him is both a model for how we are called to love and a revelation of God's self-offering of control out of love. This model for how you and I are to love is not an invitation to masochism or some sort of foolhardy and dangerous behavior. Instead, it is an example of our willingness to accept both the suffering and the joy that comes with love. This revelation of God's self-offering or sacrifice of control tells us a great deal about who Jesus Christ is and what God is like.

In abstract theological ways, medieval thinkers developed a tradition of describing God as impassible, literally one that is incapable of suffering (from the Latin *impassibilis* with that same root word *passio*). While the purpose of this sort of description was to highlight the utter transcendence of God, distinguishing the human or created realm from that which is totally unique to God, there are some obvious problems with taking this sort of claim or description of God too far.

Suffering was seen, at least classically, as a weakness. Because human beings and other aspects of creation are finite and imperfect, they succumb to the experiences of loss and pain, of suffering and the involuntary removal of control. And we can confidently say that if God so chose, God would presumably never suffer. However, as we have already discussed above, the choice to love—and true love is always a choice—is a decision to surrender certain control and embrace the suffering that even a little boy can recognize as at times inaugurating total agony.

Love also bears great joy, fulfillment, and completion, but the suffering side of passion is inherently part of the reality. The love God freely exercised, the love that led to the greatest event in the history of creation—the Incarnation—is summarized in the often-quoted verse from the Gospel according to John: "For God so loved the world that he gave his only Son, so that everyone who believes in him may not perish but may have eternal life" (3:16). What that surrender of control out of love means on the part of God is described in further detail in the Letter to the Philippians:

> Let each of you look not to your own interests, but to the interests of others. Let the same mind be in you that was in Christ Jesus,
>> who, though he was in the form of God,
>>> did not regard equality with God
>>> as something to be exploited,
>> but emptied himself,
>>> taking the form of a slave,
>>> being born in human likeness.
>> And being found in human form,
>>> he humbled himself
>>> and became obedient to the point of death—
>>> even death on a cross. (2:4–8)

This ancient hymn has been described as "kenotic" (from the Greek word *kenosis*, meaning "to empty oneself"), revealing the pattern of love that God demonstrates in the life and actions of Jesus Christ. The self-emptying is the surrender of control, the willingness to risk much for the sake of another, and to lay down one's life for one's friends.

Elsewhere in the Gospel we have other glimpses of how Jesus expresses to his disciples and to us today how he understood the relationship between love and suffering. One example is in the Gospel According to John where he anticipates what is coming for him in the form of the cross and connects it to the love God has shown in his own life. Jesus then instructs his followers to make a similar connection and to accept the call to self-offering that exemplifies what it means to truly love as God has and intends for us.

> As the Father has loved me, so I have loved you; abide in my love. If you keep my commandments, you will abide in my love, just as I have kept my Father's commandments and abide in his love. I have said these things to you so that my joy may be in you, and that your joy may be complete.
>
> This is my commandment, that you love one another as I have loved you. No one has greater love than this, to lay down one's life for one's friends. (John 15:9–13)

Not only does this self-offering, this surrender of control that comes with the embrace of love, lead to suffering—such as laying down one's life for one's friends—but there is also the return of joy, and complete joy for that matter, which is something that only God can give. But, are we willing to drink from that cup from which Jesus drank (Matthew 20:22)? Are we willing to embrace our divine call to love and, therefore, suffer?

We, of course, have the free will to simply walk away. However, those who walk away from love, perhaps because of the fear of being hurt and suffering, never grow into the most mature or complete versions of who they were created to be. Rohr explains that true love and suffering are ultimately paths toward transformation. These fundamental experiences of human existence open us up, oftentimes in ways that surprise us, to seeing the world in a new way. We grow as integrated people through the experiences of such powerful surrendering and losing of control. Rohr notes that "when you are inside of great love and great suffering, you have a much stronger possibility of surrendering your ego controls and opening up to the whole field of life."[9] Who we are is in part discovered in whom we love and how we suffer.

What Jesus's decision to accept the call to love and suffer, to drink from the cup handed to him, to accept the sentence from Pilate and walk willingly up to Calvary, does for us is show us that our love is about more than our personal gratification and that our suffering is more than about our individual pain. Life does indeed open up to us in those moments because, through those experiences of surrendering and losing control, we come to see our relationship to God, others, and the rest of creation in a new light. We come to know ourselves and become who we really are when we stop trying to control each and every aspect of our lives (and the lives of others, for that matter).

The renowned Trappist monk and author Thomas Merton understood the meaning of love modeled after Christ's example. In his mid-twentieth-century writings, he lamented the commercialization and self-centeredness that shaded so much of what people in his day considered to be love. In his own way, he offers something of an explanation for why people in the modern era might be less willing to "drink from the cup" of love and suffering that Jesus did and invites his followers to do likewise. He writes:

> The trouble with this commercialized idea of love is that it diverts your attention more and more from the essentials to the accessories of love. You are no longer able to really love the other person, for you become obsessed with your own package, your own product, your own market value.... For many people what matters is the delightful and fleeting moment in which the deal is closed. They give little thought to what the deal itself represents. That is perhaps why so many marriages do not last, and why so many people have to remarry. They cannot feel real if they just make one contract and leave it at that![10]

How much more prevalent is this sense and misunderstanding of love today? The basic problem with this sort of popular notion of love is that those who want to believe in it wish to separate it from the other side of passion, which is suffering, and therefore seek to maintain all control at all times. Isn't this really what so many people want? More control? Merton addresses this desire for control head-on:

> The plain truth is this: love is not a matter of getting what you want. Quite the contrary. The insistence on always having what you want, on always being satisfied, on always being fulfilled, makes love impossible. To love you have

to climb out of the cradle, where everything is "getting," and grow up to the maturity of giving, without concern for getting anything special in return. Love is not a deal, it is a sacrifice. It is not marketing, it is a form of worship.[11]

Like Richard Rohr, Merton sees authentic Christian love as a path toward growth and maturity. It requires the surrender of personal control and the desire for self-gratification, and it challenges us to move beyond the superficial to encounter the true depth of our human condition and divine grace.

While the Passion with a capital *P* reflects the unique self-offering of Jesus on the cross, his embrace of complete love and suffering, every instance of our human response to God's call to follow Christ, to love one another wholeheartedly, is in a sense a passion with a little *p*. As Merton says above, love is a sacrifice and, insofar as we can talk about Jesus's death on the cross as a sacrifice, our living passionately in this world is similarly an experience of self-surrender and embrace of relationship.

Christian Discipleship and Our Sharing in the Passion of Christ

There has been a danger in the past of preachers and writers trying to explain, or even explain away, the words from and the action of Christ on the cross in such a way as to make sense of it all. The contemporary American theologian Stanley Hauerwas cautions us against falling into that spiritual trap as he offers his own reflections on these famous final words.

Hauerwas explains, "It is my conviction that explanations, that is, the attempt to make Jesus conform to our understanding of things, cannot help but domesticate and tame the wildness of the God we worship as Christians."[12] This sort of Christian dead end occurs when we project onto the Passion (with a capital *P*) what would help us make sense of the events, words, and actions of God in Jesus Christ. In doing so, we move beyond learning from the words of Christ to putting our own words into his mouth.

Instead of focusing on putting forward our explanations, as Hauerwas warns, my suggestion is that we open up our hearts and minds to the real possibility that the Holy Spirit continues to speak to us through the words of Christ on the cross. Can we imagine that what Jesus says in the Gospels stirs something up in the hearts and minds of the contemporary hearer? Can we take what Scripture scholars have identified as key themes and points in these words and understand them in light of today's passion (with a little *p*), which is the everyday experience of the human family's love and suffering?

Can the words from the cross offer us a framework by which we can better appreciate the disparity between the love of popular culture and the Christian love of self-surrender? Can the power of these words rightfully shock us into compassion—which literally means "to suffer with"—for those whose pain and sorrow is unknown to us, ignored by us, or made possible by our actions or omissions? Can we drink from the same cup from which Christ drank?

One aim of this book is to offer a series of reflections, a Lenten retreat of sorts, that allow women and men in the modern world to look at the Seven Last Words from the cross through a new lens in order to challenge all of us to enter into the Passion of Christ in a meaningful way. No definitive explanations will be given, but many possible points of experiential resonance will be suggested. It is at this intersection of the words of Christ with the experiences of Christians that one finds the centrality of social justice in the living of authentic Christian discipleship.

While the term *social justice* has received negative connotations in some circles in recent years due to certain media misrepresentations of the tradition, the vocation of all Christian women and men to work toward the common good, protect the dignity of all human life, strive toward ending violence in all forms, and providing for the welfare of all people remains integral to who we are as bearers of the name Christ.

As I mentioned in the preface above, so often the good news of the Gospel becomes nothing more than a muted version of an overused tune. "We've heard this one before," we might complain in our silent ways, which is simply a reflection of our complacency in the spiritual life and stagnation along the way of our Christian journey. By highlighting the ways in which our Christian discipleship is dependent on our sharing in the passion of Christ, it is my hope that this Lenten retreat—this invitation to take time and reflect on the Seven Last Words of Jesus—serves as a source of renewal and motivation.

FRANCIS OF ASSISI AND THE CROSS OF CHRIST

Another aim of this book is to offer a uniquely Franciscan take on the Seven Last Words. While this is in no way an academic study of Francis of Assisi or the broader Franciscan tradition's take on the Passion or the cross of Christ, there is much to be gleaned from the spiritual and theological resources of the Franciscan tradition in helping us to understand these Seven Last Words. To talk about Francis's view of the cross is perhaps more complicated than one might at first presume it would be.

Unlike the subsequent devotional focus on the crucifixion and the cross of Christ apart from the rest of the Christian story, something that is made strikingly clear in the phenomenon of Mel Gibson's 2004 film *The Passion of the Christ*, Francis always viewed the cross from an incarnational standpoint. For Francis, as the French scholar Damien Vorreux has noted well, the central theological thread for his spiritual outlook was the Incarnation of Christ. However, "the Incarnation is not limited to Christmas," Vorreux illustratively reminds us.[13] That God became human remains the key focus of Francis's view of Jesus's life and death. "The human condition accepted by Christ includes death. It is thus, in all its far-reaching implications and its later development, that Francis envisaged the Incarnation as leading up to and including the cross."[14]

For Francis it is the love of God, the self-offering and surrender of control that comes with the Incarnation, that is at the heart of what it means to talk about the suffering of Jesus on the cross.

This sense of giving up control is seen in the way the Franciscan scholar Zachary Hayes describes the place of the cross in the spiritual worldviews of Francis and Bonaventure.

> When we look at the mystery of Christ, however, both for St. Francis and for Bonaventure, this evokes quite a different sense of the divine. When we think of the historical origins of Jesus, the poor circumstances of his life, the tragic historical ending on the cross, we must ask in what sense this is truly the incarnation of divine love. For both St. Francis and for Bonaventure, such historical realities point our attention to the humble, tender elements of the world in order to discover there important signals of the presence of the divine. How can one look at the figure on the cross without asking: What is the nature of creative and redemptive love? What is truly creative power?[15]

What it means to talk about love is laid out for us on the cross. And it is this sense of divine love—made concrete in the Incarnation and completed in the suffering on the cross—that was so transformative in Francis's own life.

We must not forget how the legend of Francis's initial conversion to religious life begins before the cross in the form of the now-famous San Damiano crucifix. Vorreux describes that experience of Francis before the cross and how the young would-be saint would understand what was depicted before him:

Waiting for him over the altar was a great Byzantine Christ that Francis particularly liked because it represented a redeemer at once friendly and triumphant. This savior did not seem to say to the faithful, "Look how I suffered for you!" but "Look how much I love you!" It was "a Christ of peace and persuasion."[16]

It is not a God who is vindictive, vengeful, sadistic, or punishing that speaks to the heart of Francis and calls him forth to live more deliberately his baptismal vocation to follow the Gospel, but a God of love. It is a God who suffered on the cross precisely *because* of love, not despite it. And this love, this *passion* for humanity, touched the life of Francis in a permanent, life-altering way.

After Francis's death, Bonaventure will talk about the "transformative power of love."[17] Love is what moved the heart and mind of the saint from Assisi, and it is love that is the greatest force for change and good in our world. The cross, therefore, was not a sign of sin and death, but a sign of the tremendous power of love that speaks through the centuries, across all times and places, to the daily human experiences of true love.

Hayes recalls how in so many ways, often in the subtleness of the ordinary day-to-day, people are changed and shaped by the love of those and for those with whom there is a relationship. So too we are changed, if we are likewise open to the possibility, by the love experienced in relationship with the God who loves us so much that God desires to be with us as one like us. Hayes writes:

"The life of grace and the imitation of Christ are a process of responding to the divine offer and the example of Christ. And the human person is changed in that process. We become like what we love."[18]

In the case of Francis of Assisi, he indeed became like what he loved. If the cross was instrumental in the early conversion of Francis, then it was also formative in his daily life and represented in a unique way at the end of his earthly journey. Most people are familiar with Francis's stigmata, the miraculous reception of the five wounds of Christ, near the end of the saint's life.[19]

Theologians have suggested that one of the ways we can understand the marks of the crucifixion on the body of Francis is that he so conformed his life to that of Christ, that he was so committed to embodying the Gospel, that he was so open to being transformed by the love of God, the saint became like what he loved: Christ. That this was made manifest in a physical way is rare, but the exemplary manner of Francis's own way of living the Gospel, seen even to this day by the millions of women and men still inspired by his example, demonstrates the transformative ability of love in a very powerful way.

As it happens, the early biographers of Francis's life make note that the gift of the stigmata was in fact rather painful. In other words, one of the effects of the transforming power of God's love seen physically in the wounds on Francis's body was suffering.

A particularly Franciscan view of the cross of Christ and the Lord's Passion first requires that love and suffering not be separated but, like the meaning of the word *passion* itself suggests, these two sides of the coin remain connected in our reflections.

Second, the Franciscan tradition always calls us to return to the Incarnation and the tremendous love that led to God's becoming one like us to live as one among us. Any reflection on the cross should not be disconnected from the Incarnation, or to put it another way: Good Friday has as much to do with Christmas as it does with Easter. When we dwell on the suffering without remembering the love that provided the condition for the possibility of the cross, we end up distorting the meaning of our faith.

Finally, a Franciscan approach recognizes the inherent transformative power of love. As with all relationships, both parties must be open to love and to be loved. With God in Jesus Christ, the openness is always already there, the onus falls to us to respond to that love. In our response, our openness can lead to transformation and change the way we see the world, the way we treat one another, the way we care for the rest of creation, and the way we relate to our Creator.

How to Use This Book

This little book is designed to be used by you in the way that you see most fit. There is no right or wrong way to proceed with considering the chapters that follow. Each chapter is designed with the same structure to help you reflect on the last words of Christ from the cross in a new and relevant way, drawing on the traditions and insights outlined in this introduction.

Every chapter begins with the traditional phrase (the "word") and the extended passage of Scripture from which the phrase is taken. You will find that the texts come from a variety of Gospel sources, and some of them are rather closely located to one another in the Bible, while others are relatively self-contained.

Following the presentation of the traditional phrase and the broader scriptural context, a reflection is presented that focuses on how that saying of Jesus might speak to today's Christian audience in new, relevant, and timely ways. What might it evoke in the reader? What is happening in our world that resonates with the message of Christ? Dedicated to highlighting the dimensions of social justice in the Gospel generally and in these sayings specifically, each reflection also contains some resources from the Franciscan tradition.

At the end of each chapter, you will find a series of reflection questions and an original prayer. These are for your use, but you shouldn't feel obligated to draw on them if they don't speak to your experience and reading of the reflection. Perhaps you might wish to reflect on or discuss your own interpretation of the Seven Last Words or raise new and different questions. You might also feel moved to compose or spontaneously offer a prayer inspired by a given Scripture passage and chapter. While the ordering of the Seven Last Words follows the traditional sequencing, you should allow yourself to move around from word to word as you desire.

However you decide to draw on this resource, it is my hope that you might find this book enlightening and thought-provoking. May your Lenten journey and your lifelong Christian pilgrimage bring you closer to the transformative love of God and the suffering that such love entails.

THE FIRST WORD

Father, forgive them, for they know not what they do.

—Luke 23:34

✿

asking for grace everyday

SCRIPTURE

Two others also, who were criminals, were led away to be put to death with him. When they came to the place that is called The Skull, they crucified Jesus there with the criminals, one on his right and one on his left. Then Jesus said, "Father, Forgive them; for they do not know what they are doing." And they cast lots to divide his clothing. And the people stood by, watching; but the leaders scoffed at him, saying, "He saved others; let him save himself if he is the Messiah of God, his chosen one!" The soldiers also mocked him, coming up and offering him sour wine, and saying, "If you are the King of the Jews, save yourself!" There was also an inscription over him, "This is the King of the Jews." (Luke 23:32–38)

REFLECTION

Ignorance is bliss. And what you don't know can't hurt you. Right? These phrases have eased the minds of many over the years, clichés though they may be.

The truth that rests at the heart of these adages is the very real desire so many people have to not know. Some don't want to know about suffering and sorrow in the world. Others don't want to know the truth that *all* people have inherent dignity and deserve to be loved, regardless of who they are or what they've done. Still, so many others don't want to know that the way many live in this country—that is, the United States of America—is indeed an exception to the global rule. Poverty is something that only the comfortable can afford to ignore, because it is the lifelong reality for everybody else.

Yet, if ignorance is bliss and what you don't know can't hurt you, then all things are well—unless, of course, they're not, which is what seems to be hinted at in the first of Jesus's words from the cross. For if ignorance is bliss and what you don't know can't hurt you, then there would be no need to associate forgiveness with ignorance, and the Gospel might have ended another way.

Some have read this line of Jesus—"Father, forgive them, for they know not what they do"—as consisting of an action and an explanation. Jesus asks his Father for forgiveness on behalf of those who are killing him, and he does this because the people don't realize what they are doing. There is something comforting about this interpretation of the text, a sort of relief for those of us who recall what happened during that Good Friday when the Son of God was executed like a criminal. "Surely," we say to ourselves, "God can't hold these people responsible, because they don't realize who it is they are killing." However, there is another way to look at these first of the last words of Christ.

This other way to look at Jesus's words is to see a request for forgiveness *because* the people didn't realize what they were doing. The transgression, the action that requires God's forgiveness, isn't just the crucifixion of an innocent man, thereby granting the murderers a get-out-of-jail-free card because they don't know what they are doing. No. The two seemingly distinct things are really connected. The people require God's forgiveness *because* of the crucifixion *and* their willful ignorance: "Father, forgive them, *because* they don't know what they are doing!"

Do we live in the world in such a way that we too need forgiveness for what we do not know? Each time we gather together to celebrate the Lord's Supper and hear the Word of God at Mass, we say as much when we beg God's pardon for "what we have done and what we have failed to do." I would suggest, that ignorance in many cases is not bliss, but is in fact sin; and what we don't know may still not hurt us, but it might very well hurt others.

It is easy to overlook the things "we have failed to do" and instead devote our attention to our wrongful thoughts and actions in the world. I am reminded of the tragic story of Hugo Alfredo Tale-Yax, who died in a terrible event that took place in Queens on the morning of April 18, 2010. Here, in part, is how *The New York Times* reported the story.

> Hugo Alfredo Tale-Yax's last act may have been helping a
> woman who was having an argument with another man
> last Sunday morning in Queens. But his last hour or so was

spent as a curiosity for people passing him on the street as he lay face down in blood after being stabbed several times.

Mr. Tale-Yax, 31, was pronounced dead by medical workers who responded to a 911 call around 7:20 a.m. on April 18. The police confirmed the authenticity of surveillance video on *The New York Post's* Web site that shows dozens of people walking by Mr. Tale-Yax, who was homeless, lying on the sidewalk at 144th Street and 88th Road in Jamaica. After more than an hour, the video shows one man shake Mr. Tale-Yax before turning him over to reveal the wounds....

The police were not sure if the woman knew what happened to Mr. Tale-Yax, but they said it was possible she knew the suspect. The police expressed hope that news coverage of the killing will prompt her to realize and identify the suspect.[20]

For whom does Jesus, from the cross, ask forgiveness in this event? The words of the Lord seem to suggest, at least to me, that the "dozens of people" that walked by, stepped over, overlooked and ignored the dying thirty-one-year-old man are need of God's forgiveness. *They knew not what they were doing.*

Some will say, "But surely it is not their fault, for these people may not have seen him, may not have known what was happening." Such an observation is not untrue. Many, or perhaps even most, of those who were videotaped by a nearby security camera may not have seen the man dying at their feet, and therefore, an argument might be made in their defense. Yet, what sort of culture do we tolerate or even promote in our neighborhoods and country that allows us to bypass another human person sprawled on a sidewalk without even the slightest expectation to see if he or she is in need of help?

While some might not have seen the dying man, others certainly did and willfully passed on by without concern or regret. Some were captured on the security camera stopping and looking, curious but uninterested in assisting. Still others, uncertain of what had happened or who was in need, decided not to know, chose instead to maintain their ignorance over compassion, and failed to do something to save the life of Mr. Tale-Yax. One phone call to 911 would have been enough.

St. Francis of Assisi was, for the better part of his young life, not unlike those New Yorkers who walked passed the dying man on the street. As a homeless man, Hugo would have become accustomed to being ignored. Poor, outcast, and living at the margins of society, his experience can be likened to that of the sick, misunderstood, and poor of Francis's day. Outside the medieval city walls of Assisi lived those who were not welcome to live among the rest of society. These were people like the lepers, whose illness was misunderstood and who, in turn, were rejected and treated as if already dead.

The law of the time required that they make their presence known when approaching others—those not cast out of society—so that the otherwise "regular people" could turn away and avoid being subjected to the at times grotesque reality that was the lived experience of the lepers. They were shunned, ignored, and rejected, and that behavior was commonplace, expected, and prescribed; not unlike the way the homeless are treated in our own cities and towns today.

Francis of Assisi readily admits that, up until the beginning of his conversion experience, he found lepers to be disgusting. Francis, at the end of his life, recalled how God had changed his heart so that he could be a brother to those he most despised. In his last *Testament*, Francis wrote:

> The Lord gave me, Brother Francis, thus to begin doing penance in this way: for when I was in sin, it seemed too bitter for me to see lepers. And the Lord Himself led me among them and I showed mercy to them. And when I left them, what had seemed bitter to me was turned into sweetness of soul and body.[21]

For Francis, the eventual changing of heart and mind, coming to see sweetness in the experience of relationship with those whom he previously despised, rejected, and ignored was of such great importance in his life that it is how he began his final reflections on his deathbed. Yet this conversion, this turning away from selfishness and willful ignorance toward those most vulnerable in the world, did not happen overnight.

The early biographers of St. Francis, people like Thomas of Celano and St. Bonaventure, went to great effort to remind us of the way in which Francis was at first repulsed by the lepers. Early in his second biography of Francis, titled *The Remembrance of the Desire of a Soul*, Thomas wrote:

> Among all the awful miseries of this world Francis had a natural horror of lepers, and one day as he was riding his horse near Assisi he met a leper on the road. He felt terrified and revolted, but not wanting to transgress God's command and break the sacrament of His word, he dismounted from his horse and ran to kiss him. As the leper stretched out his hand, expecting something, he received both money and a kiss. Francis immediately mounted his horse and although the field was wide open, without any obstructions, when he looked around he could not see the leper anywhere.[22]

Some have speculated that it was Christ who appeared to Francis disguised as a leper and perhaps that is why Francis was able to overcome his fear of the other and the willful ignorance he espoused. Thomas of Celano makes it clear, however, that it wasn't until afterward that the mysterious leper disappears. What might have been implied in telling this experience is that one finds Christ among the despised, voiceless, and forgotten of the world. We have to move beyond that which we wish to ignore and forget about: embrace the seemingly un-embraceable, love the unlovable, and dare to know what we most fear and wish to leave unknowable.

The ignorance exhibited by those who nailed Jesus to the cross, who mocked a dying man and who stood by in silence strikes us as abhorrent today. *If only they would have known.* But the truth hidden in the senseless death of a young homeless man in Queens, New York, and the embrace of a physically repulsive leper in Francis's lifetime is that Christ continues to be found in our world. Do we pass him by on the street, subjecting him to the humiliating and public death of a victim ignored? Or do we get off of our high horse like Francis, who on some level still wanted to ignore the suffering of another, to embrace what we don't understand and fear the most?

Sometimes what we have failed to do doesn't confront us in the same way that a dying man on a sidewalk or a leper outside of Assisi might. We live in a very insular society, and as a result, much of our reality is as closed off as we would like it be. In a country filled with isolating cul-de-sacs, neighborhoods insulated from the troubles, concerns, and reality of the outside, there are people who remain equally shut off from the lives of others. It is tempting to stay in our own worlds. It is simpler and cleaner and safer. But is that why Jesus died on the cross and spoke these words of forgiveness? So that we could live in our own worlds, ignoring the plight of others in the human family?

The challenge for us today is the same as it was for St. Francis more than eight hundred years ago: to get off our horse and meet the needs of our brothers and sisters in this world. What began with a young man in his twenties overcoming his fear of a people he grew up with the right and privilege to ignore and despise, turned into one the greatest life stories of one following Christ.

Francis discovered that ignorance is not bliss but something to overcome and that what he didn't know was in fact hurting others. He didn't need forgiveness, because he knew exactly what he was doing. How about you?

REFLECTION QUESTIONS

- What, for me, is the most significant aspect about this first of the Seven Words?

- What are some of my own experiences of being ignored by other people? What did that feel like? How might understanding this help me deal better with some of the seemingly unimportant people in my life?

- Who are some of the people in my life that I find myself ignoring—willfully or unintentionally? At home? Among friends? At school? At work? Among relatives? Where I live? In my faith community?

- What are some of the ways I think I can work on developing better relationships with some of these people?

PRAYER

Jesus, our crucified Lord,
you know us better than we know ourselves.
Help us to see the ways in which we not only
act out in selfishness, greed, or shortsightedness,
but also in those ways we choose to ignore,

forget, and step over aspects of our lives and others
for which we need forgiveness.

Help us to shed the desire to not know
and instead lead us on the path toward moving beyond
that which we wish to ignore and forget so we may
embrace the seemingly un-embraceable,
love the unlovable,
and dare to know what we most fear and wish to leave unknowable.

From the cross you prayed that we may be forgiven,
teach us to pray for the strength to forgive others and ourselves.

For the times we have hurt others through our own self-interest,
for the times we continue to choose blindness to others' needs
instead of sight,
for the times we forget that we must forgive the trespasses of
others as we ourselves are forgiven,
have mercy on us.

May we never say, "If only we had known,"
and instead seek out the lost, lonely, poor, and forgotten.

May we, in kissing the lepers of our lives, find you.

And in finding you, recall that ignorance is not bliss,
and what we might not know may in fact be hurting others.

We make this prayer in your name.

Amen.

Is true forgiveness

THE SECOND WORD

Today you will be with me in Paradise.

—Luke 23:43

൚

SCRIPTURE

One of the criminals who were hanged there kept deriding him and saying, "Are you not the Messiah? Save yourself and us!" But the other rebuked him, saying, "Do you not fear God, since you are under the same sentence of condemnation? And we indeed have been condemned justly, for we are getting what we deserve for our deeds, but this man has done nothing wrong." Then he said, "Jesus, remember me when you come into your kingdom." He replied, "Truly I tell you, today you will be with me in Paradise." (Luke 23:39–43)

REFLECTION

In between the lines much is happening during these four verses that capture Jesus's conversation with the two criminals on the cross shortly before his death. While there are several ways to look at this text, something about this three-way conversation strikes me as containing truths far-too-often overlooked.

Take the first criminal for instance. Here is a guy who, presumably like his fellow criminal, committed some serious crime. We can presume this because the man is being executed, and we are told this because his fellow death-row inmate—the other criminal, not to be confused with Jesus, who was also sentenced to capital punishment—says as much when he rebukes the first criminal with the address: "Do you not fear God, since you are under the same sentence of condemnation? And we indeed have been condemned justly, for we are getting what we deserve for our deeds, but this man [Jesus] has done nothing wrong" (Luke 23:40–41).

The first criminal, like the soldiers who nailed Jesus to the cross, seemingly taunts Jesus while he faces the same fate. "Are you not the Messiah? Save yourself and us!" However, in what might ultimately be an honest request, although likely laden with sarcasm, the question-and-command combination of his remark is perhaps the most-succinct depiction of the most-common prayer ever uttered by the human race. When we are scared, pushed to our breaking points, unsure of our futures, doubting our abilities, or generally confused about life, doesn't our prayer sound a lot like the question we hear in the Gospel? How often is the first criminal's question our own? *If you are really there, God, then let me find a job...then save my dying father...then help me!*

Faced with the most challenging of life's circumstances—death, in this case—the first criminal asks the question that so many of us find at the tip of our tongues when the going gets tough.

Sure, we might not get going, as the saying goes, but we sure get blaming and challenging, and at times, we are obstinate. "Jesus," we cry out, "*do something!*"

How is this different from what the apparently sarcastic criminal asks from his cross? And, by the way, what makes him sarcastic? Is it the fact that we cannot stand to recognize the perfectly human tone of his question, a helplessness and desperation that so many of us can recall in our darkest hours? Or is it because he is rebuked by his sidekick, that other criminal sentenced to die as painfully and as publicly as the other two, that we immediately presume that this criminal is doing anything less than being honest in his question to Jesus? Whatever the reason, I wonder now if the first criminal is as much a bad guy as we might usually make him out to be.

Ah, yes, but it is the second criminal who gets the affirmation of his impending reward. At least, that is how the author of Luke's Gospel tells the story. Before Jesus is able to respond to the first question, the second criminal jumps in to rebuke the first criminal for his ostensibly rude question. What we see is not Jesus acting as mediator, settling this disruption that has appeared on Golgotha, but Jesus responding to the request of the second criminal who, after speaking to the first criminal, redirects his comments to Jesus: "Remember me when you come into your kingdom."

Jesus responds, not to a man's singular cry for his own salvation like the first criminal, but to the exclamation that resembles what Jesus taught his own disciples when they asked for a lesson on prayer: *Thy kingdom come.*

What Jesus speaks from the cross is an echo of the truth that he spoke earlier in his ministry. How does one pray to God? Not in the way demonstrated by the first criminal.

I am increasingly less convinced that the first criminal's words in any way resembled the mockery of the soldiers and shameless bystanders. No, I believe that the first criminal was honestly trying to pray in the face of the most horrific experience of his life. But the only way he knew how to pray was in the form of a challenge, a demand. It is the prayer of those who think that God is a miracle worker who intervenes in this or that instance, and when such a request appears to go unanswered, it is God's fault and no one else's.

That is so often our prayer. This is, many times, the only prayer people know. *Please, please, please, God!*

Yet the second criminal speaks something else here. The words uttered from the other side of Jesus's cross are words as complex as the first criminal's demanding plea. The second criminal's prayer is both an Act of Contrition, seeking to acknowledge his own wrongdoing (*forgive us our trespasses...*), and a request. While the first criminal is making a demand, the second criminal's request takes the form of surrender instead of control. And this is, in some basic way, a reflection of the second criminal's openness to love—a willingness to surrender control for the sake of another, for the sake of something greater.

Whereas the first criminal knew what he wanted, the second criminal asks for what is needed. Earlier Jesus had taught his disciples that they should pray with humility, behind closed doors, asking that "thy kingdom come, thy will be done, on earth as it is in heaven." So too the second criminal makes this prayer his own as he faces his own sins and finally, perhaps for the first time in his life, seeks that God's will be done.

Paradise is not found on the beaches of a Caribbean island or in some mythic garden from the book of Genesis. Paradise is where God's will is done, where the kingdom of God is more than breaking in. It is the very reality of our existence with God without the gloss of our own selfish desires, without our own obsessive need for control. It is the location—not so much in time and space, but in experience—where, like God, who is more and more *Deus pro nobis* ("God for us"), we live more and more as women and men for others. As the Our Father says so clearly, as the second criminal says implicitly, God's kingdom—this paradise about which Jesus speaks—is found when his *will is done*.

St. Francis of Assisi knew this and realized that the effort to follow God's will above one's own desires was how he and his brother friars should live. In the first Rule or way of life for the Franciscan friars, St. Francis tells the brothers:

> Therefore, let us desire nothing else,
> let us want nothing else,
> let nothing else please us and cause us delight
> except our Creator, Redeemer and Savior,
> the only true God
> Who is the fullness of good,

all good, every good, the true and supreme good,

Who alone is good,

merciful, gentle, delightful, and sweet,

Who alone is holy,

just, true, holy and upright,

Who alone is kind, innocent, clean,

from Whom, through Whom and in Whom

is all pardon, all grace, all glory

of all penitents and just ones,

of all the blessed rejoicing together in heaven.[23]

The kingdom of God is made present in the experience of those who seek God's will above all else in this life. The second criminal, facing the end of his earthly existence recognized this truth and, having admitted his wrongdoing, proclaims this truth of which Francis speaks.

And Jesus responds: Amen.

Paradise, or the kingdom, is also a reality that is not off in some distant future, but is, as Jesus says, here "with me today." It is easy, with the quickly impending death of the three being executed, to mistake Jesus's words as simply referring to the next life—which, he also surely meant. However, what Jesus is also affirming in his response of "Amen," or "truly," or "so be it,"—whichever translation is used in your particular Bible—is the truth that we are called not just to *say* the prayer Jesus taught us to the Father, but to *live* it in our daily lives. *Thy will be done!*

It seems to me that our focus on the Passion of the Lord,

especially his death on the cross, has distracted many of us from the last parable the Gospels show us: the parable, as I call it, of the two criminals. It is the parable of how to pray, which is reflected in how we live. So which criminal are you? How is it that you pray?

REFLECTION QUESTIONS

- What do I think is the most significant aspect of this chapter?
- What are some of the circumstances in my life when I've found myself wondering if God is there for me? What does that feel like when it happens? Do I think I'm a bad person because I find myself doubting the presence or grace of God in my life?
- When I take time to really think about prayer in my life, what do I think is truly at the heart of it? What does it mean to surrender in the sense described in this chapter? What does the phrase the "will of God" mean for me in my life?
- The goal of life (or the will of God) and the effect of prayer, for any disciple of Jesus, are to build up the kingdom of God. In other words, as a Christian, I need to make the presence of God more real in the world that I live in. What are some of the ways that I think my life truly reflects this?

PRAYER

Good and Gracious God,
You know our human frailty, weakness, and sin.
At times, we can easily forget who we are and who you are:
The God who has been, is always, and will remain there for us.

Forgive us for the times when we have been quick to demand,

slow to understand,

and even slower to live in such a way as to proclaim:

thy kingdom come.

Like the first criminal nailed to the cross beside Jesus,

we can let our fear, our doubts, and our need for control

take over, and,

in doing so,

we can lose sight of what is most important in our lives,

now and at the hour of our death.

Like the second criminal nailed to the cross beside Jesus,

give us the strength to embrace your love,

to surrender our control,

and face the suffering that might come our way.

May our prayer, like the second criminal's,

be a prayer of contrition and a request;

May we truly recognize our wrongdoing in life,

while embracing the future you hold before us.

Following the Lord,

it is our prayer to become instruments of peace in our world

so that we might indeed live in such a way that

paradise might arrive and your kingdom come,

on earth as it is in heaven.

We make this prayer in your name.

Amen.

The Third Word

Woman, behold your son.

—John 19:26

∽⟶

When the soldiers had crucified Jesus, they took his clothes and divided them into four parts, one for each soldier. They also took his tunic; now the tunic was seamless, woven in one piece from the top. So they said to one another, "Let us not tear it, but cast lots for it to see who will get it." This was to fulfill what the scripture says,

"They divided my clothes among themselves,

and for my clothing they cast lots."

And that is what the soldiers did.

Meanwhile, standing near the cross of Jesus were his mother, and his mother's sister, Mary the wife of Clopas, and Mary Magdalene. When Jesus saw his mother and the disciple whom he loved standing beside her, he said to his mother, "Woman, here is your son." Then he said to the disciple, "Here is your mother." And from that hour the disciple took her into his own home. (John 19:23–27)

REFLECTION

"Good Friday has seen the disintegration of Jesus's community," the former Master General of the Dominican Order Timothy Radcliffe once observed. "Judas has sold him; Peter has denied him, and most of the disciples have run away. All Jesus's labours to build a little community seem to have failed. And then, at the darkest moment, we see this community coming into being at the foot of the cross. His mother is given a son in his closest friend, and the beloved disciple is given a mother."[24]

Imagine what it must have been like for Jesus at this moment. Having spent his adult life announcing the kingdom of God, preaching the love of the Father and the forgiveness of sins, healing the broken and brokenhearted, his good works and his holy life have led him to be sentenced to death like a common criminal. Just the night before he was at table with his closest friends, sharing with them his final earthly meal, showing them how to call to mind his life and real presence. To the garden they went, Jesus and those he loved, and at the moment he most needed friendship and support, they disappointed him. Jesus is arrested there some time later and once it becomes clear that he will be kept captive, his friends run away for fear of the same fate.

Nearly everybody is gone now. And those who remain are those who have always been there. They include the first to believe in Jesus and the ones for whom the fear of a similar fate does not outweigh their loyalty and love. At the center of the small group mourning and supporting the crucified Jesus is Mary, his mother.

At the beginning of John's Gospel, from which we hear these words from Jesus to his mother and friend spoken, it is Mary who first confesses belief in the mission and ministry of her son. At the wedding reception at Cana, it is not Jesus who announces his first miracle, nor is it the band of disciples he has just assembled, but Mary whose faith precedes that of all else.

> On the third day there was a wedding in Cana of Galilee, and the mother of Jesus was there. Jesus and his disciples had also been invited to the wedding. When the wine gave out, the mother of Jesus said to him, "They have no wine." And Jesus said to her, "Woman, what concern is that to you and to me? My hour has not yet come." His mother said to the servants, "Do whatever he tells you." Now standing there were six stone water jars for the Jewish rites of purification, each holding twenty or thirty gallons. Jesus said to them, "Fill the jars with water." And they filled them up to the brim. He said to them, "Now draw some out, and take it to the chief steward." So they took it…. The steward called the bridegroom and said to him, "Everyone serves the good wine first, and then the inferior wine after the guests have become drunk. But you have kept the good wine until now." Jesus did this, the first of his signs, in Cana of Galilee, and revealed his glory; and his disciples believed in him. (John 2:1–11)

She said to those staffing the banquet, "Do whatever he tells you," and thus began the mighty deeds of the Lord that signaled the in-breaking of the kingdom of God.

Flash-forward to the end of the story: what began as a joyful celebration of new life in marriage has ended in the most painful and humiliating of deaths, a tragedy that even Shakespeare could not have conjured. His abandonment on the cross anticipates the reality of discipleship his followers, but for a few, would face in some manner at some points in life.

When Jesus invites us to be his disciples saying, "If any of you want to become my followers, let them deny themselves and take up their cross daily and follow me" (Luke 9:23), it is not necessarily the safe, comfortable, and sterile use of metaphor with which some have described this passage away in retrospect. Those who envision the cross Jesus speaks about as a figurative device likely forget the next line in the Lord's address to us: "For those who want to save their life will lose it, and those who lose their life for my sake will save it" (Luke 9:24).

My guess is that most of the disciples ran away because they wanted to save their lives. They, in the face of real danger, could not deny themselves to take up their crosses, so they were forced to deny Jesus and leave him alone to carry his cross. They didn't understand, but really—when we're honest with ourselves—do we?

Those few friends and family members who stayed behind and perhaps risked their own lives for the sake of their friend and Lord have denied themselves to follow Jesus. And where the fleeing disciples feared the loneliness of abandonment and death that Jesus faced, those who remained discovered something quite the opposite. In Jesus's words to his mother and his friend John we see the promise of community. Just as Jesus says before the Passion narrative in Matthew's Gospel, "for where two or three are gathered in my name, I am there among them" (Matthew 18:20), he brings together those who have gathered at the foot of his cross and assures them that they will have each other.

I have heard it said that what is at the core of this exchange— "woman behold your son, son behold your mother"—is the patriarchal cultural context of first-century Palestine at play, where a woman had to be attached in some way to a man. And with Joseph presumably already dead and Jesus now dying, he wanted to be sure Mary was secure in the community. He loved and trusted the "beloved disciple" enough to establish that connection for her. It seems that on one level this may very well be the case, but there is more going on here than simply accounting for the widowed and would-be childless Mary of Nazareth.

The beloved disciple is also the "faithful disciple" who has followed Jesus to the end, carrying his cross daily and offering his life for the sake of the kingdom. The faithful disciple is entrusted with a mother who, in true maternal form, will care for and guide John as if he were her son. The same is true for all the faithful disciples. Those who are willing to carry their crosses daily and risk their lives for God's sake can trust in the enduring community of discipleship and the care that Mary—the new Eve, or mother of all humanity—provides through her prayers and intercession.

Scholars such as Elizabeth Johnson, in her book *Truly Our Sister: A Theology of Mary in the Communion of Saints*, help us to see how the entrusting of Mary and the beloved disciple to each other provides a glimpse into Jesus's desire for all those who would follow him in generations to come.

> The symbolic theological importance of the crucifixion scene in [the Gospel of] John surfaces in the idea that at the end of his life Jesus brought into being a community in the very Spirit that flowed from him on the cross. Two great figures without a name appear, the mother of Jesus and the beloved disciple. Both were historical persons but are not named here because they are functioning as symbols of discipleship. Standing by the cross they are turned toward each other by Jesus's words and given into each other's care.... The formula "Behold" or "Look" indicates that a revelation is to follow, such as John the Baptist's cry "Behold the Lamb of God" (John 1:36) and Pilate's statement "Behold your King" (John 19:14). Beholding each other in a new relationship, the mother of Jesus and the beloved disciple mark the birth of a new family of faith founded on the following of Jesus and his gracious God. The mother/son language indicates that, just as in the Synoptic scene with the mother and the brothers, Jesus is reinterpreting family in terms of discipleship.... In a word, the mother and the beloved disciple are representative of a larger group, the church.[25]

If we look closely, we too can see in this moment of intimacy spoken from the darkness of the crucifixion is the light of the Spirit's work in uniting the community of believers known as the Communion of Saints. In this life and in the life to come, all who believe are united as one family in the Spirit; like mother, like brother, like sister, like child to all. "Because of the cross and from the moment of the cross," the Scripture scholar Francis Maloney explains, "a new family of Jesus has been created. The Mother of Jesus, a model of faith, and the disciple whom Jesus loved and held close to himself are one as the disciple accepts the Mother in an unconditioned acceptance of the word of Jesus."[26] So too Mary becomes our mother when we accept the word of Jesus unconditionally, which is no small task.

For Francis of Assisi, accepting the word of Jesus unconditionally meant following the good shepherd. Francis once wrote:

> Let all of us...consider the Good Shepherd Who bore the suffering of the cross to save His sheep. The Lord's sheep followed Him in tribulation and persecution, in shame and hunger, in weakness and temptation, and in other ways; and for these things they received eternal life from the Lord. Therefore, it is a great shame for us, the servants of God, that the saints have accomplished great things and we want only to receive glory and honor by recounting them.[27]

Francis knew that a temptation for Christians in his time and in our own would be to water down as much of the call to discipleship as was necessary to comfortably bear the name of Christ. Yet even in his own community Francis admonished his fellow friars to live a life of true discipleship, not simply by recounting the laudable lives of those who came before us, but to imitate those models of holiness by living up to our fullest vocation to follow Christ.

As part of the communion of saints, all of us are connected to the body of Christ, like the beloved disciple was connected to Mary at the foot of the cross. Johnson has elsewhere succinctly explained what the communion of saints means for us: "The Communion of Saints is a Christian symbol that speaks of profound relationship. In traditional usage it points to an ongoing connection between the living and the dead, implying that the dead have found new life thanks to the merciful power of God. It also posits a bond of companionship among living persons themselves who, though widely separated geographically, form one church community."[28]

Both Sts. Francis and Clare of Assisi recognized the importance of what happened at the cross as a model for Christian life. They also recognized the connection that the cross has to our formation of community, friendship, and the communion of saints. As Franciscan theologian Ilia Delio explains:

> What Clare and Francis saw in the mystery of the crucified Christ was not a violation of human dreams and hopes but the God of self-giving love. It was this God who grasped their lives. They were convinced that suffering out of love for another, following the example of the Crucified Christ, leads to happiness, unity and peace because this is the path

of friendship with God. Their notion of friendship was not based on needs and wants but on the desire for mutuality, fulfillment and happiness that they believed could only be found in God. And they discovered this path of friendship in something we usually reject—the cross.[29]

Like the two criminals on either side of Jesus, our choice is between what we want and what is needed, between the will of our own desires and the will of God. To follow Christ means a willingness to surrender all, even to the point of losing one's life for God's sake.

To surrender all is to embrace the vulnerability and openness of love, while the concomitant and alternative side of that passion is the inevitability of suffering. To follow Christ, in its simplest articulation, is to love. And love we must. We are created for and called to love to the point of suffering, perhaps even suffering to death.

Today, as perhaps it has always been, this is a challenging invitation. At first those who knew Jesus best, many of his disciples and friends, could not bear the responsibility of the call to follow him. It was only later that they came to recognize the community he had formed in them, so that filled with the Holy Spirit in the Upper Room, they could look around at one another and behold the mother, the brother, the sister, and the child each was to one another in Christ.

As you look around at the people in your life, who is it that you behold? Are you willing to risk losing your life of self-interest to gain the life God desires for each of us?

REFLECTION QUESTIONS

• What is the most important aspect of this chapter for me?

• If I'm honest with myself, what are some of the times in my life when I saw that I was unable to "deny myself and take up my cross?"

• What are some of the circumstances and situations that I've encountered in life—or that I currently experience—in which I am asked to selflessly give of myself? In what specific ways have my experiences in doing this helped me to appreciate the presence of other people in my life, or to "see the promise of community?"

• Francis and Clare "were convinced that suffering out of love for another, following the example of the crucified Christ, leads to happiness, unity and peace because this the is path of friendship with God." What does this statement mean for me? What are some examples or particular relationships in my own life that have helped me appreciate the reality that friendship with God is manifest in life-giving human relationships?

PRAYER

God of community and love,
there are many times in our lives
when we are too quick to abandon Christ on the cross.
Like those disciples who feared for their lives,
things great and small cause us to fear for ours.
Help us to see the two sides of your Son's passion,
the love and suffering that Jesus reveals to us,

models for us,

calls us to live.

Open our eyes to the truest meaning of bearing the name "Christ,"

so that we too may strive to love as you love,

while embracing the suffering that such true love entails.

We offer our gratitude for the community formed that day beside
the cross:

formed out of great love,

formed amid great suffering.

We offer our gratitude, too, for the love of Mary in our lives.

She continues to offer us care and concern

as our sister in the Communion of Saints.

She continues to model for us the way of Christ.

She understands our love and our suffering.

We ask for the grace to build up,

and not runaway from,

the community you formed at the foot of the cross.

We make this prayer in your name.

Amen.

THE FOURTH WORD

My God, my God, why have you forsaken me?

—Mark 15:34

⸎

SCRIPTURE

When it was noon, darkness came over the whole land until three in the afternoon. At three o'clock Jesus cried out with a loud voice, "Eloi, Eloi, lema sabachthani?" which means, "My God, my God, why have you forsaken me?" When some of the bystanders heard it, they said, "Listen, he is calling for Elijah." And someone ran, filled a sponge with sour wine, put it on a stick, and gave it to him to drink, saying, "Wait, let us see whether Elijah will come to take him down." Then Jesus gave a loud cry and breathed his last. And the curtain of the temple was torn in two, from top to bottom. Now when the centurion, who stood facing him, saw that in this way he breathed his last, he said, "Truly this man was God's Son!" (Mark 15:33–39)

REFLECTION

What's in a name?

The entire meaning of the line, "My God, my God, why have you forsaken me?" comes down to understanding what the name of God means. Who is the one to whom Jesus addresses his cry from the cross? Why has he chosen these words?

Jesus makes the prayer of Psalm 22 his own as he dies on the cross. These are in fact the last words that Jesus utters in the Gospel of Mark, tragic in a sense, yet frequently misunderstood. What sounds like a cry of abandonment and despair reflects only part of what Scripture scholars believe Christ was expressing. For, as we had seen earlier during the suffering in the garden, even the Anointed One of God struggles to make sense of his experience, praying that this suffering that has come along with his love might pass.

> They went to a place called Gethsemane; and he said to his disciples, "Sit here while I pray." He took with him Peter and James and John, and began to be distressed and agitated. And he said to them, "I am deeply grieved, even to death; remain here, and keep awake." And going a little farther, he threw himself on the ground and prayed that, if it were possible, the hour might pass from him. He said, "Abba, Father, for you all things are possible; remove this cup from me; yet, not what I want, but what you want." (Mark 14:32–36)

Jesus's words in the garden and then again on the cross express an honest, painful lament. But the words from the cross are not entirely his own. Like the author of Psalm 22 and all those who have invoked the lines of the ancient Hebrew prayer afterward,

Jesus uses his own tradition to articulate his experience, his suffering and his loss for original words.

> My God, my God, why have you forsaken me?
>> Why are you so far from helping me, from the words of
>> my groaning?
> O my God, I cry by day, but you do not answer;
>> and by night, but find no rest. (Psalm 22:1–2)

If one was to stop at these two opening verses, indeed the fate of the Lord would seem marred by despair and his final cry would be one of hopelessness and abandon. But lament in the Hebrew tradition does not always end in misery, and this particular psalm must be understood in its fullness.

Theologians are quick to point out that if the author of the Gospel of Mark intended for the narrative about the life and death of Jesus of Nazareth to be a tragedy, a different title would have been selected because as it is, the title of the book—the oldest written Gospel among the four—bears the name "the *Gospel* according to Mark," that is: "the *Good News* according to Mark."[30] Jesus giving up at the end is hardly good news.

So what is this line all about?

In order to better understand, we must return to the full text of the Psalm. Immediately following the two opening verses of clear lament there is a switch in style and tone. While the psalmist begins in the present, concerned about the pain, suffering, and loneliness felt in the moment, the prayer moves forward to recall the ways in which God had been there for the psalmist's ancestors and how God did not abandon them in their past.

> Yet you are holy,
>
> enthroned on the praises of Israel.
>
> In you our ancestors trusted;
>
> they trusted, and you delivered them.
>
> To you they cried, and were saved;
>
> in you they trusted, and were not put to shame. (Psalm 22:3–5)

And what follows is one of the most honest, yet difficult, prayers that one can find in all of Scripture. The author goes back and forth from describing the state of things in the midst of suffering and seeming abandonment to recalling the way in which God has always remained faithful and has not failed to seek the best for the chosen people. Take the following verses for example:

> But I am a worm, and not human;
>
> scorned by others, and despised by the people.
>
> All who see me mock at me;
>
> they make mouths at me, they shake their heads;
>
> "Commit your cause to the LORD; let him deliver —
>
> let him rescue the one in whom he delights!"
>
> Yet it was you who took me from the womb;
>
> you kept me safe on my mother's breast.
>
> On you I was cast from my birth,

and since my mother bore me you have been my God.

Do not be far from me,

for trouble is near

and there is no one to help. (Psalm 22:6–11)

This sense of the immediacy of suffering, pain, and anxiety alternates with the reassurance that the psalmist knows God is not far away, God has not abandoned the psalmist's ancestors, and God will be there in the future. This sense of assurance amid suffering arises from the psalmist's understanding of the name of God.

Over the centuries, some people have misunderstood the name of God. In the theophany recorded in the book of Exodus—the revealing of God's name to Moses on Mount Sinai—we understand that this name is signified by four letters: YHWH, which will come to be translated centuries later as "I AM."[31] But this is, I believe, a matter of something rather important being lost in translation.

The general acceptance of this meaning and translation over the centuries has led to an inadvertent shift in the way many people understand who God is. The earliest versions of this experience of Moses interacting with God would have been passed on orally and only later written down. It wouldn't be until much, much later that the notion that YHWH could be understood as meaning "I AM" would appear on the scene, largely the result of the influence of Greek philosophy on interpreting Scripture.

Those who originally heard this story of God and Moses would understand the complexities and richness of God's name that would eventually be lost in translation. It is a name that *describes* God, not limiting God as the more philosophical reading of "I AM" so often does. A more accurate rendering of God's name in translation reads: "I am the one who will be there for you." It bespeaks relationship and future. It tells the whole story of God's relationship with humanity and all creation in miniature.

When Moses goes to Pharaoh on behalf of God's people, he is to say that the "One who journeys with the chosen people" has sent him. We see this in the often overlooked next verse in the book of Exodus where God explains to Moses who God is in another, more relational way.

> God spoke to Moses, "Thus shall you say to the Israelites:
> The LORD, the God of your fathers, the God of Abraham,
> the God of Isaac, the God of Jacob, has sent me to you.
>
> This is my name forever;
> this is my title for all generations." (Exodus 3:15)

The name of God is precisely who God is, a God who is with us, who loves us, and who will be there for us. This is made even clearer in the next line as God continues to speak to Moses.

> Go and assemble the elders of the Israelites, and tell them:
> "The LORD, the God of your fathers, the God of Abraham,
> Isaac and Jacob, has appeared to me, saying: I have given
> heed to you and to what has been done to you in Egypt. I
> declare that I will bring you up out of the misery of Egypt,
> to the land of the Canaanites, the Hittites, the Amorites, the

Perizzites, the Hivites and the Jebusites, a land flowing with milk and honey." (Exodus 3:16–17)

When we don't just stop with "I AM" but read on to hear God explain who God is to Moses, we come to see that God cares for us and is concerned about the way we are treated by unjust powers and in oppressive circumstances. God is not some abstract deity who lives in the clouds, nor is God a disinterested authoritarian. God is the Creator who is head over heels in love with humanity and seeks what is best for creation out of that love and concern.

Keeping in mind who God is by recalling God's name helps us to understand what Jesus is saying on the cross. He begins as the psalmist does, recognizing the conditions of human suffering, of defeat, and of rejection, but it is after this lamentation that we begin to see the emergence of the "good news" arise over the horizon. Like the full text of Psalm 22, Jesus's death and resurrection express a reality that is complicated, emotionally moving, and yet joyful.

Death does not have the last word. And that is indeed the good news.

From the perspective of the cross near the point of death, there is little one can do but acknowledge the tremendous suffering that has occurred. Women and men all around the world recognize this cry of lament. The suffering, abuse, and marginalization of our sisters and brothers happen in myriad forms and in many places. Still, the good news—the Gospel—comes in remembering who God is.

God is the one who *will be there for us!* God is the one *who is concerned and cares for us!* God is the one who, as we pray in Psalm 34, *hears the cry of the poor!*

The Brazilian theologian and former Franciscan friar Leonardo Boff, when reflecting on the event of Jesus's cry of Psalm 22 from the cross, sees a sign of hope amid suffering, which is indeed good news for those who work for justice in our world. Boff wrote:

> There are countless prophets of sacred causes that espouse the rights of the poor. Some are known; the vast majority are anonymous. They all share the impotence and the helplessness of Jesus on the cross. They are asked to accept the most difficult assignment: to hope against hope, to love what does not seem to be present to them, and to believe in what they cannot see. They are asked to endure the worst plight a human being can experience: to die feeling abandoned by the God for whom they lived and sacrificed their lives.
>
> Still, they do not abandon God. They surrender themselves to God in complete confidence. In total inner emptiness they cling to the nameless Mystery that is infinitely beyond them. For this mysterious God holds the secret meaning of all their failed quests, of all the absurdities of history. To die like this is to share his redeeming mystery, which will go on through history until the world reaches its end and fulfillment in the liberation of the last sinner who opens to God's mercifulness.[32]

Suffering is a condition of human existence. Our imperfection, our weakness, and our finitude all but guarantee that we will suffer in some form during our time on this earth. That God, through the Incarnation, understands the reality of human suffering and the feeling of abandonment experienced on the cross helps us to situate our prayer and realize that God does in fact live up to the name. God continues to be the one who will be there for us, especially when we, like Jesus in his life and ministry, work on behalf of justice in the world, yet still do not abandon God.

What Psalm 22 means for us is that God still lives up to who God is even when we struggle to remember who we are. Amid the pain and suffering of our lives, when it becomes difficult to see our own goodness or the goodness of the world, we can look to Christ, who in his suffering remembers who God is and reveals the truth that death does not have the last word.

REFLECTION QUESTIONS

- When I consider my most intimate moments of prayer, what name do I give to God? What do I like to call God? How does this name describe my relationship with God?

- What are some of those special times and moments when I have been certain that God has been there for me, that is, when I have been deeply aware of God's love for me and concern about me and the rest of humanity?

- In this chapter we read, "Suffering is a condition of human existence." At times, our own pain and suffering blinds us to "seeing our own goodness or the goodness of the world." Yet, in the Incarnation, we see that God understands the reality of this human condition. What are some of those times when I have suffered or felt abandoned only to realize that God really is close to me, and that God knows my suffering in a personal way?

PRAYER

Most High, Glorious God,
open our eyes to see your presence,
open our minds to know that you are there for us,
open our hearts that we might love like you.
Life can be very difficult,
wrought, at times, with pain and suffering.
Control is taken away without warning,
and we are left to cry out:
"My God, My God, why have you abandoned me?"
Yet, you give us the grace, if we are willing to accept it,
to see what the psalmist saw,
to recognize what Jesus knew,
and to recall that you are never far away.
In our times of suffering,
may we follow the example of Jesus and the psalmist;
but may we also serve as a source of comfort
and consolation to others in their suffering.
May we never let the fear of suffering
stand in the way of our calling to love and work for justice.

May we come to better understand who we are
in coming to better understand who you are.
We make this prayer in your name.
Amen.

THE FIFTH WORD
I thirst.

—John 19:28

❧

SCRIPTURE

After this, when Jesus knew that all was now finished, he said (in order to fulfill the scripture), "I am thirsty." A jar full of sour wine was standing there. So they put a sponge on a branch of hyssop and held it to his mouth. (John 19:28–29)

REFLECTION

During the summer of 2008 I lived in Cochabamba, Bolivia. Staying in a nearly five-hundred-year-old friary in the center of the city, I lived with my Spanish-speaking Franciscan brothers while I studied Spanish by morning and got to know the community and practice my language skills by afternoon.

If you don't know much about Bolivia, you're not alone. Most people from the United States are unfamiliar with this country, as well as its people, history, and culture. For starters, it is the poorest of the countries in South America. It is not a destination spot or a vacationer's paradise, like so many other locations in Central and South America, although the country's beauty is incredible, and its people are warm and welcoming. Bolivia is rich in many natural resources, yet its postcolonial experience has been a trying one, marred by corruption, political instability, and a whole host of other problems.

One such problem has been the issue of water.

In the United States, unlike most of the world, we have the excessive luxury of clean water delivered into most of our homes in most parts of the country. Few of us have to think twice about taking a glass to the kitchen sink, filling it up with water from the faucet, and drinking it plainly. In fact, so spoiled are we by the infrastructure and water systems here in the United States of America that many purchase pitcher-like filters and install additional filtering devices right to the tap when such measures are unnecessary, only to perhaps improve the taste or make already potable water slightly more palatable to the American taste.

In the United States clean drinking water delivered to our kitchens is but the beginning of the ways in which we unthinkingly use water daily. Not only does that clean water come through our taps and into our drinking glasses, but it also comes through a labyrinth of pipes to our bathrooms, filling toilet bowls and spraying through showerheads. We water our lawns and gardens, fill children's pools, and wash our cars, windows, and sidewalks. Even our pets benefit from the clean water we pipe through our cities and villages, whether it is in the form of a drink to quench a kitten's thirst or a bath to clean a dirty puppy.

We don't have to think about the quality of our water, we just use it. But as I came to realize during my time in South America, we also really abuse it.

Bolivia is not the only country that does not share the luxury of clean, available water found in the United States and other wealthy nations. I have visited several places in the global south during which time I could not drink the water from kitchen or bathroom sinks: Peru, the Dominican Republic, and Mexico, to name a few. But it was in Bolivia that I came to first appreciate the seriousness of the phrase of Jesus on the cross, "I thirst," and the absurdity with which so many of the wealthiest populations on this planet—who make up a tiny percentage of the global population—abuse and waste clean water.

I came to this aqua epiphany through the experience of another, which came in the form of a story. The story was one told to me by an older friar who has lived in Bolivia for most of his adult religious life. Originally from the United States, he entered the friars with my province and wanted to serve as a missionary in South America. He went to Bolivia as a young man and has lived there ever since.

In the beginning there weren't enough Bolivian friars to form an independent province, but over the years friars would come, and numbers slowly increased. There came a time when the Bolivians could form their own community, and it was then that this friar decided that his heart and his home was Bolivia, so he joined the newly formed community.

When I arrived in Cochabamba with my friar classmate, Steve, this friar met us at the airport along with several other expatriate American friars. Some time later, long after I had settled into my new, if temporary, home, this friar and I were talking about the differences between the United States and Bolivia. It came up in conversation that not that many years ago, he had returned to Cochabamba after spending a few weeks back in the United States visiting his family.

A woman from the Franciscan parish came up to him one day after Mass, and because she had heard that he had just returned from the U.S., she asked if he might be willing to answer a question.

"Padre," she said, "I know this is going to sound ridiculous, but because you've just spent some time in the United States, I thought you might be able to clear up a matter that has been a hot topic of debate among my family for some time now." Unsure of where this was going, he asked her to go ahead with her question, and he would try his best to answer. She continued, "a friend of my sister's claims that in the United States the people are so wealthy that they use clean water in the toilets. I've told her that this is impossible and one of the craziest things that I've ever heard, but we finally agreed that we'd ask you to put this matter to rest."

My fellow friar stopped the story there, at which point I asked him what he said to her. He said, moved by shame and the scandal of the disparity between some of the wealthiest and poorest people in the world, he lied. He couldn't bring himself to tell her the truth. He had no explanation for why some people—like many in the United States—live in such a way that they can flush their waste down the drain with water that people elsewhere on the globe would literally die to have, people who would gladly have dipped a cup in the toilet bowl of any of the thousands of homes in the United States.

It is usually only when we lack something that we need that we come to realize how we have taken that thing for granted for so long. Are United States citizens bad people because their toilet water can be consumed as drinking water? No, I don't think so. But the question, "How can some members of the human family have so very much and others have absolutely nothing?" should come up in our reflection more often than it does.

In an early Franciscan document that depicts Francis and the early brothers having a conversation with evangelical poverty personified as a noble lady, we read this line: "Poverty is the only thing that everyone condemns so that it cannot be discovered in the land of those living comfortable."[33] In many ways we, those who live in the United States and other nations of the so-called Global North and Global West, live in a land of comfort. Granted, not everybody does, but comparatively, most of us live a lifestyle that never really forces us to face the reality that there are men and women in this world who die daily because they do not have the food, shelter, or water—the most basic of necessities—that they need to keep themselves or their families alive.

I can say that I have never truly been thirsty. Perhaps the closest I've come to true thirst occurred last summer when I was running a fifteen-kilometer road race, and due to dehydration and some other medical issues, I collapsed. Treated by a medical team and taken to the hospital, I was given the live-saving fluids and medications needed to keep me going and prevent my heart from stopping. Yet, there are those whose daily lives present the challenge of survival because something as simple as water to drink is not available or affordable.

Too often interpretations of this line of Jesus from the cross have been overly spiritualized. Some like to say that there is a spiritual connection between the episode where Jesus expresses his dying thirst and is given unsatisfying drink and the earlier exchange in John's Gospel when the Samaritan Woman hears about Jesus's water that will be given and "those who drink will never thirst again" (John 4:13). There is a temptation for many reading this passage from Scripture to quickly look at Jesus's thirstiness in a spiritual sense and conclude that it is somehow symbolic of the waters of eternal life. There is a temptation to gloss over the real and powerful human suffering that comes with someone dying of dehydration, suffering real, life-ending thirst. But the waters of eternal life mean little for those who die waiting for the waters of basic earthly life.

Timothy Radcliffe makes the keen observation that, "because our bodies are 98 percent water," we might better view "dehydration [as] the seeping away of our very being, our substance.

We feel that we ourselves are evaporating. So often the last desire of those who are dying is for something to drink."[34] In a rather literal sense, there is perhaps nothing more dehumanizing than to let someone die of thirst, to evaporate away, to diminish in existence. Unlike so many other challenges of this world that threaten human safety and security, to prevent death by thirst requires nothing more than a little clean water.

A 2002 article from *The New Yorker* magazine by staff writer William Finnegan summarizes well the problem of access to clean water around the globe.

> More than a billion people have no access to clean drinking water, and nearly three billion live without basic sanitation. Five million people die each year from waterborne diseases such as cholera, typhoid, and dysentery. This enormous, slow-motion public-health emergency is, in large measure, a result of rapid, chaotic urbanization in the nations of the Global South. Traditional water sources have been polluted, destroyed, overtaxed, or abandoned.
>
> Annual rainfall is not always a measure of water wealth. Poland, for instance, gets plenty of rain, but its lakes, rivers, and groundwater are so polluted that it has as little usable water as Bahrain. Arid regions with the means to pay (Southern California, the Persian Gulf States) already pipe water in from wetter areas. New technologies are being hurriedly developed: huge fabric bags holding millions of gallons of fresh water are being hauled by barges across the

Mediterranean, and there are businessmen in Alaska who believe that the state's earnings from fresh water will eventually dwarf its earnings from oil.[35]

The words "I thirst" uttered from the cross are echoed in the cries of those who go without adequate supplies or access to clean drinking water. These words also evoke the teaching of Jesus found at the end of Matthew's Gospel, when the Lord says to his followers that it is when they feed the hungry, clothe the naked, give something to drink to the thirsty that they are in fact serving him. How is it that we can quench the thirst of the Lord on the cross in the lives of those who are dying from lack of water today? What does the cry "I thirst" from the cross mean for us in terms of the ecological crises of our own day?

Jesus continues to thirst in the lives of those hanging on the crosses of poverty and oppression. What is it that we have done or *have failed to do* to serve the least among us? Do we work to alleviate the suffering of our sisters and brothers, helping to fight against systems of injustice that allow for nearly half the human race to go without basic sanitation and clean water? Or do we flush our resources down the toilet and water our lawns with what could sustain the least among us without a second thought?

Jesus said, "I thirst." What do you say, what do you *do* in response?

REFLECTION QUESTIONS

- To repeat the challenge of this chapter: "How is it that we can quench the thirst of the Lord on the cross in the lives of those who are dying from lack of water today?" What are some of the ways that I might be able to appreciate the actual thirst of other people, respond to it, give something to drink, and thus serve the Lord?

- The lack of clean, fresh, and healthful water is a serious ecological problem. The world thirsts. At the same time, the lack of water can be a metaphor for all the systems of injustice that afflict poor, powerless and alienated people today. The world thirsts for more than simply water. What are some of the things that I do, or can decide to do, to help fight systemic injustice? Or, as we read earlier in the chapter: "What do I say, what do I do in response?"

PRAYER

God of life,

we are grateful for the many gifts that you have given to us.

We celebrate the life-giving quality of the rest of creation,

the water that nourishes us,

the plants and animals that feed us,

the materials that shelter us,

the stars that guide us,

and the sun that energizes the planet.

We recognize that,

as privileged citizens of our particular time and place,

that we do not always live as those appreciative of what we have received.

For those times when our

taking advantage,

taking for granted,

and taking beyond our need

have caused others to suffer for our lack of love and awareness,

we ask for forgiveness.

We also ask for the strength, courage, and insight

to work for justice and equity in our world.

May our recognition of your generosity in our lives

spurn us on toward actions that empower the human family

to guarantee that God's creation not be squandered for the sake

of a few,

but that we sustainably support one another and share in our bounty.

May we become prudent stewards of your many gifts

and not thoughtlessly waste water, food, and other resources.

May we respond to your Son's cry of thirst

with lives of peacemaking and just action.

We make his prayer in your name.

Amen.

THE SIXTH WORD

It is finished.

—John 19:30

❧

SCRIPTURE

When Jesus had received the wine, he said, "It is finished." Then he bowed his head and gave up his spirit. (John 19:30)

REFLECTION

There is a fine line between beginnings and endings. With one the other inevitably follows. That's why college graduations are called commencements: what at the same time marks the completion of several years of study also marks a new beginning, a new chapter in the life of the graduate.

Central to the Christian message of the cross—the very reason that followers of Jesus hang these signs of death penalty and torture on walls and places of worship over the centuries—is that in earthly death, one doesn't find just an end, but one finds also a beginning. It is, as the Franciscan tradition refers to the anniversary of the death of St. Francis of Assisi, a *Transitus*—from the Latin word indicating a passing over from this life into the next.[36]

What has, in a sense, finished has also just begun.

Curiously, the meaning of the Greek word used in the Gospels that captures what Jesus cried out from the cross is not as clear-cut as we might at first think—which, I'm sure, is no accident. Reflecting this fine line between beginnings and endings, what is generally translated into English as "it is finished," might better be translated as "it is fulfilled."

The word *finished* has a terminal sound to it. Some Scripture scholars believe that *tetelestai*, the Greek word the author of John's Gospel uses, is more triumphant than it is evocative of surrender. Francis Moloney explains: "Climaxing these [earlier scriptural] indications of fulfillment, Jesus cries out '*tetelestai*' (v. 30a), an exclamation of achievement, almost of triumph. The task given to him by the Father (cf. [John] 4:34; 5:36; 17:4) has not been consummately brought to a conclusion."[37] The exclamation isn't something from which one needs to shy as much as it is an embrace of all that has come before, yet points toward the future where we are now to go. It is a climactic exclamation—*it is fulfilled!*—just like college graduation, but it is also the announcement of what is also beginning.

No one understood this better than St. Francis. His biographer Thomas of Celano tells us that while Francis was very sick and near the end of his life, he spoke to his fellow brothers about how they were to look at this point in the saint's life and in their lives.

> He used to say: "Let us begin, brothers, to serve the Lord God, for up until now we have done little or nothing." He

did not consider that he had already attained his goal, but tireless in pursuit of holy newness, he constantly hoped to begin again.

He wanted to return to serving lepers and to be held in contempt, just as he used to be. He intended to flee human company and go off to the most remote places, so that, letting go of every care and putting aside anxiety about others, for the time being only the wall of the flesh would stand between him and God.[38]

As Francis came to the end of this earthly journey, he echoes the words "It is finished" proclaimed by Christ on the cross. His words are not helpless, regretful, or empty in their recognition of one chapter in the pilgrimage of life. Instead, he expresses— perhaps in a way more fully than Jesus's simple "It is finished"— that, while the other friars and sisters were crying about the imminent loss of their leader in religious life, Francis wanted to remind them of what it means to announce a commencement, a completion, a fulfillment, and a beginning: It is not a time of sorrow or loss, but a time to refresh and renew one's commitment to the Gospel, to live as one in the kingdom, and to continue to serve the Lord with redoubled intent.

In this way, Francis's mirrored expression of those words from the cross—"Let us begin, brothers, to serve the Lord God, for up until now we have done little or nothing"—is an invitation to make Christ's words—"It is finished"—our own over and over again in life. There is a sense in which the call to serve the Lord found in Francis's deathbed announcement is a commentary or explanation of what Jesus might have meant in his own cry from the cross, for to proclaim that "it is fulfilled" in a Christian context is to necessarily assert, "Thy will be done." Is it no wonder then that Francis, as he lay dying, asked that the reading from the Gospel of John at the Last Supper be read to him?

At his own *Transitus* from this life to the next, Francis sought to recall what it was that he committed himself to so many years earlier. "To live according the Gospel of our Lord Jesus Christ." That life was one of service in solidarity. That service in solidarity is demonstrated on the eve of the Lord's own death, while at table with those he loved. The reading Francis begged to hear is this:

> Now before the festival of the Passover, Jesus knew that his hour had come to depart from this world and go to the Father. Having loved his own who were in the world, he loved them to the end. The devil had already put it into the heart of Judas son of Simon Iscariot to betray him. And during supper Jesus, knowing that the Father had given all things into his hands, and that he had come from God and was going to God, got up from the table, took off his outer robe, and tied a towel around himself. Then he poured water into a basin and began to wash the disciples' feet and to wipe them with the towel that was tied around him. He came to Simon Peter, who said to him, "Lord, are you going to wash my feet?" Jesus answered, "You do not know now what I am doing, but later you will understand." Peter said

to him, "You will never wash my feet." Jesus answered, "Unless I wash you, you have no share with me." Simon Peter said to him, "Lord, not my feet only but also my hands and my head!" Jesus said to him, "One who has bathed does not need to wash, except for the feet, but is entirely clean. And you are clean, though not all of you." For he knew who was to betray him; for this reason he said, "Not all of you are clean."

After he had washed their feet, had put on his robe, and had returned to the table, he said to them, "Do you know what I have done to you? You call me Teacher and Lord—and you are right, for that is what I am. So if I, your Lord and Teacher, have washed your feet, you also ought to wash one another's feet. For I have set you an example that you also should do as I have done to you." (John 13:1–15)

After the reading was completed, Francis "told them to cover him with sackcloth and to sprinkle him with ashes, as he was soon to become dust and ashes."[39] The last words Francis heard came to form a summary of the saint's entire life: service and solidarity. Francis wasn't just one who served others, but lived with and for them in a way that reflected the relationship Jesus demonstrated with all people. This is how Francis understood the *Vita Evangelica*, the life of the Gospel, and this is how he wished those who were to come after him would live.

Francis lived his life as if every day was a proclamation of "It is finished; it is fulfilled." He strove to obey the words of Jesus after the Lord had washed the feet of his followers and said, "For I have set you an example that you also should do as I have done to you." Francis then left those who were following him to do likewise.

It can be difficult to tell the difference between beginnings and endings. Perhaps one of the strongest lessons in Jesus's words from the cross, those words lived in the life of St. Francis, is that we must not be as concerned about *our* time as we are about *God's* time. In God's time beginnings and endings are one in the same, because God's time is not so much a matter of minutes, hours, and days as it is about a way of living in the world. The way we mark the passage of our life is not the same way that God marks our time. It is when washing the feet of others, the giving of ourselves for the sake of our brothers and sisters, that we live according to God's time.

The time of the world is a time that sees the crucifixion of an accused criminal on a Roman cross as an end. The time of the world is a time that sees a blind, poor man dying naked in medieval Italy as an end. Yet the time of God is a time that sees in all things the potential for a new beginning, a reminder that life is more than an economy of checks and minuses, of winning and losing. God's time is a time of fulfillment that makes little sense to the world, for what is logical is replaced by what is kingdom-oriented, and as St. Paul reminds us, this way of thinking appears as foolishness and remains a stumbling block to the worldly (1 Corinthians 1:18–31).

People like Jesus of Nazareth and Francis of Assisi were fools for God, abiding in time that was not limited by the priorities of popular culture and society. To be a disciple today, to live up to the claim that you or I are willfully following the one who cried, "It is finished," from the cross means to risk being foolish in the eyes of the world in order to be wise, loving, and renewed in the eyes of God. It means living in a time that prioritizes relationship and second chances, of starting over again to serve the least among us, of valuing what it is that God values.

But do you have the time?

REFLECTION QUESTIONS

- The phrase "It is finished" can have a very negative connotation, like "I'm finished; I'm sunk; it's all over now but the crying; is this all there is? Yet, as we read in this chapter, the words are really much more subtle than that. Retranslating this phrase as "It is fulfilled" invites us to reframe the question to something like: "What else is there?" "Who else can I be?" "What else can I do?" These are questions that are full of hope and expectation. How is God calling me to continue to build up the kingdom today, especially as I grow in my understanding that all time is God's time?

- How can I use my time to better serve "the least among us?" Who are "the least among us" in the worlds that I live and work in? What are some of the changes that I can make in my life to make this service possible?

PRAYER

God of all time,

You call us out of the ordinariness of our everyday lives

to see the world anew in your time.

Help us to respond to your call to see in all things:

both a completion *and* a new beginning;

both an end *and* a renewed start;

both sadness *and* joy.

While our time marks your death on a cross as an end,

your time marks the *Transitus* from one life to the next.

Enflame in our hearts a desire to see in life and death

the *Transitus* and transformation your life, death, and resurrection

have brought forth in the world.

Your time is a time of fulfillment that makes little sense to the world,

for what is logical is replaced by what is kingdom-oriented,

and this way of thinking appears as foolishness to the worldly.

Help us to live as your fools,

willing to announce your kingdom.

Give us the strength to keep your time,

where relationships take priority

and we start over again and again

to serve the least among us.

Amen.

The Seventh Word

Father, into your hands I commend my spirit.

—Luke 23:46

❧

SCRIPTURE

It was now about noon, and darkness came over the whole land until three in the afternoon, while the sun's light failed; and the curtain of the temple was torn in two. Then Jesus, crying with a loud voice, said, "Father, into your hands I commend my spirit." Having said this, he breathed his last. When the centurion saw what had taken place, he praised God and said, "Certainly this man was innocent." And when all the crowds who had gathered there for the spectacle saw what had taken place, they returned home, beating their breasts. But all his acquaintances, including the women who had followed him from Galilee, stood at a distance, watching these things. (Luke 23:44–49)

REFLECTION

Luke has always been, hands down, my favorite of the four Gospel accounts. Now, I'm not sure if that is like a parent coming right out and saying that one of several children is his or her favorite, but it is the truth no less. There are aspects for which I admire each of the other three Gospels, but if there were a contest for Fr. Dan's Favorite Gospel, Luke would win in the overall package.

There are several unique narratives that can be found only in Luke's account. Take, for example, the most famous Marian passages in Scripture—Mary's visit to Elizabeth or the appearance of the angel Gabriel. Both of these encounters are exclusively conveyed by Luke. Throughout the Gospel one finds some of the most striking and memorable parables and sayings of Jesus. Perhaps you recognize a parable that begins with this famous line: "A man was going down from Jerusalem to Jericho, and fell into the hands of robbers, who stripped him, beat him, and went away, leaving him half dead" (Luke 10:30). It is the parable of the Good Samaritan. Or perhaps this opening line is familiar: "There was a man who had two sons" (Luke 15:11). It is the parable of the Prodigal Son.

It is not just because of the unique stories and the teachings of Jesus found only here that I like Luke's account so much. There are also more subtle aspects of the Gospel that capture my attention and continue to challenge me every day as a person of faith. The place of the poor and marginalized in Luke's version of the Gospel as well as the significance of table fellowship for Jesus's ministry and mission are important to me, calling me to be more open and accepting of others—particularly the forgotten, the voiceless, and the poor—in living the Christian life. Yet this last saying of Jesus from the cross that we consider among the Seven

Last Words speaks to me of another dimension of Luke's account that might be overlooked by those who are not paying particularly close attention.

These words from the dying Lord bespeak a closeness, intimacy, and special relationship with God. While we oftentimes conflate all of the Gospel accounts in our memory, thereby rendering a general picture of what the Gospel presents (as if it were a singular account or one book), Luke's version depicts Jesus's last words as those of someone deeply connected to God. There is a feeling of tenderness, a calm, and a grounded relationship that is not found in the versions of Matthew or Mark, the other two Synoptic Gospels, which are closest in style, content, and origin to Luke.

Scripture scholar Raymond Brown has said that there are two noticeable differences in Luke from some of the other accounts—particularly Mark, whose is the earliest written Gospel. The first is that, in Luke's version, Jesus is described in the original Greek as "crying out" (*phonein*), which is different from Mark's version, which describes Jesus as "screaming" (*boan*). What we have here is a nuanced difference, but one to which many people can relate. To scream is to lose control and react out of fear, while to cry out depicts something less violent and, possibly, more profound.

The second difference is that, in Luke's Gospel, Jesus addresses God as "Father" from the cross, which is different from Mark's version, which simply includes the address "God." In Mark's account we read the early part of Psalm 22, "My God, My God," yet Luke substitutes the address with the personal "Father." *Father, into your hands I commend my spirit.*

The subtlety is often lost on us because we are so used to hearing the words of the Passion narrative that we anticipate what will come next and rarely ever look at the different versions side-by-side. The way Luke portrays the relationship between Jesus on the cross and God the Father is not a small matter. In the other version, the Markan one that presents Jesus screaming out to God in a generic address, we see the desperation and surrender that might cause Christians to step back in confusion: *What do you mean desperation and surrender? Isn't Jesus the Son of God? Doesn't he know?* What Luke's account provides is a more nuanced appreciation for the trust and faith Jesus had even to the point of death, death on a cross.

It is this intimacy that enables Jesus to say, "Father," and it is this trust that enables Jesus to say, "into your hands I commend my spirit." Such an example naturally challenges us with a question: how do we understand our relationship with God? In whom do we trust until death, placing our entire spirit in care?

I, for one, would like to think that I could answer in a way that best reflects Jesus's model of love and trust on the cross, but honestly, I don't really know. There are so many things in life that pull at me for my love, for my trust. In the darkest moments of life, when I feel abandoned and forsaken, when I might lie at death's door, is it God whom I love and in whom I commend my spirit? Is it someone or something else? Or is it nothing at all? These last words of Christ should rock our world, should shake up our complacency and mindlessness; they are words that indict us with the ultimate charge: *Do you live in such a way as to say with your life, "Father, into your hands I commend my spirit?"*

Pope Benedict XVI, among others, has referred to Francis of Assisi as an *alter Christus* (another Christ), one who perfectly followed in the footprints of the Lord that his very life was transformed and imprinted with the marks of Christ, which we call the stigmata. Francis was one who offered us an example of what it means to live in such a way as to say, "Father, into your hands I commend my spirit," with one's whole heart, soul, and life.

In a letter addressed to all the friars, written toward the end of his life, Francis reflected on the humility of Christ who entered our world as one like us and whose sacramental presence continues to enter our world in the celebration of the Eucharist. At the end of his reflection, he highlights what it means to commend one's spirit to God.

> O wonderful loftiness and stupendous dignity!
> O sublime humility!
> O humble sublimity!
> The Lord of the universe,
> God and the Son of God,
> so humbles Himself
> that for our salvation
> He hides Himself under an ordinary piece of bread!
> Brothers, look at the humility of God,
> and pour out your hearts before Him!
> Humble yourselves

that you may be exalted by Him!
Hold back nothing of yourselves for yourselves,
that He Who gives Himself totally to you
may receive you totally![40]

Francis understood that to commend his spirit, his entire self—body and soul—to God meant that he must follow the example of Christ's humility. Like God, we too must hold back nothing of ourselves so that we can offer our whole selves—*our spirits*—to God.

How do we follow that example?

It is interesting that the first words of Jesus and the last words of Jesus in Luke's Gospel both include a reference to total commitment to God, referred to in the intimacy of "Father." The first words that we hear from Jesus come when, as a young man, Mary and Joseph discover him among the teachers in the Temple after he had been missing for some days. His first sentence is: "Why were you searching for me? Did you not know that I must be in my *Father's* house?" (Luke 2:49). His place, his work, his purpose, and mission were simply to do the will of the Father. *Thy kingdom come, Thy will be done.*

So too, when we pray as Jesus taught us, when we follow his example, when we strive to commend our spirit to God, we do so most authentically in doing the will of the Father—from the beginning until the very end.

REFLECTION QUESTIONS

- How do I understand my relationship with God? Do I understand the kind of intimacy it takes to place my trust in God until death? Do I place my entire spirit in care?

- Jesus uses the term *Father* to describe and name intimacy with God. What is that intimacy like for me? How do I name it?

- "Like God, we too must hold back nothing of ourselves so we can offer our whole selves—*our spirits*—to God." This is the language of love, of a deeply satisfying and intimate relationship. What are some of the examples in my life when I can see myself following Francis's example to commend my spirit, my entire self—body and soul—following the example of Christ's own humility?

PRAYER

Most High God,

who was called Father by Jesus,

we ask that you hear our Lenten prayer of

praise,surrender, and petition.

We praise you for the many gifts that you have given us:

the gift of life,

the gift of love,

the gift of community,

the gift of faith,

the gift of hope,

the gift of your love,

and so many others.

We surrender our control,

seeking to follow Jesus's model of humility,

while striving to love as he loved us.

We recognize that suffering comes with love,

that great love and great suffering can transform us,

but that neither experience is necessarily easy.

We offer our petition to you,

praying that we might have

the strength of our convictions,

the hope of our faith,

and the joy of that hope when times are difficult.

May we always place our trust in you

and commend our whole selves to your care.

In doing so, may we always proclaim,

in word and deed,

Thy Kingdom come,

Thy will be done!

We make this prayer in your name.

Amen.

ENDING WITH THE BEGINNING: THE FIRST WORDS OF CHRIST

For centuries we have reflected on the Seven *Last* Words of Christ during Lent, but few people have spent much time considering his earliest words in the Gospels at the same time. It might seem like these are two very different things reserved for two different liturgical seasons: the beginning is left for Advent and Christmas, while the ending is for Lent and Holy Week. But these two seemingly distinct sets of words are significantly more intertwined than we would usually imagine.

Take, for instance, the first three times that Jesus speaks in Luke's account of the Gospel. As we read at the end of the last chapter, Jesus's first words at the age of twelve bespeak a closeness to and intimacy with God that is articulated in terms of parental relationship; Jesus calls God "Father" (Luke 2:49). This is echoed throughout the story of Jesus's ministry and preaching, and repeated finally from the cross.

While we might initially think of Jesus's youthful response as that of a precocious twelve-year-old (a perspective many parents must certainly appreciate), there is a profound truth conveyed here about who God is and who we are. Jesus expresses to us, in our own human terms and from his own human experience, what the relationship is like between God and us. It is something very close, as close as that between a parent and child. Jesus, God as one like us, not only says but *lives* what was foretold in the book of the prophet Isaiah: "As a mother comforts her child, so I will comfort you" (Isaiah 66:13).

Like a mother or like a father, God knows us better than we know ourselves. This relationship is described elsewhere in Scripture as *even more intimate* than that between a mother and child, because God has said through the prophets that, "Before I formed you in the womb I knew you, and before you were born I consecrated you" (Jeremiah 1:5). To call God "Father" (or "Mother," for that matter) is a powerful statement that is for us both an address and a profession of faith.

The next time we hear Jesus speak in Luke's Gospel is when he is tempted in the desert. In response to each of the three classic temptations that the devil places before him, Jesus responds by quoting Scripture. "It is written," is the common introduction for his retort, a detail that can seem insignificant, but in fact bears an important implication. It is not Jesus alone—or each of us in our own experiences of temptation—that is the arbiter of what is right or wrong; rather, it is God through divine revelation that has made known to humanity the path we should walk. Scripture, the historical medium of God's revelation, offers us a concrete resource in coming to form our worldviews and inform our consciences.

What Jesus lays out for us in these early words in the Gospel is the importance of embracing our collective story, the narrative of God disclosing who God is over time and through the people, times, places, and events conveyed in the Hebrew Scriptures and the New Testament. Whereas Jesus, the Word made flesh, could easily have spoken some original words to combat the temptations in the desert, he instead draws from the collective story of God's chosen people, a story that he restates as his own and invites us to do the same. To speak the words of Scripture and make them our own is a powerful statement about our identity and worldview.

The third time we hear Jesus speak in the Gospel according to Luke is after he has spent the forty days and nights in the desert fasting, praying, and preparing for the start of his public ministry. Luke tells us that Jesus was then "filled with the power of the Spirit" and returned to Galilee to teach in the synagogues (Luke 4:14–15). The next thing we read is one such instance when Jesus arrived back at his hometown of Nazareth and entered the synagogue on the Sabbath.

> He stood up to read, and the scroll of the prophet Isaiah
> was given to him. He unrolled the scroll and found the place
> where it was written:
> "The Spirit of the Lord is upon me,
> because he has anointed me to bring good news to the poor.
> He has sent me to proclaim release to the captives
> and recovery of sight to the blind,
> to let the oppressed go free,
> to proclaim the year of the Lord's favor."

And he rolled up the scroll, gave it back to the attendant, and sat down. The eyes of all in the synagogue were fixed on him. Then he began to say to them, "Today this scripture has been fulfilled in your hearing." (Luke 4:16–21)

In these early words, long before the cross, we see the earliest inkling of what will eventually lead the religious and civil leaders of his time to crucify Jesus, as well as a summary of what his mission (and by virtue of our baptism, our mission) is all about: social justice.

What Jesus has been *anointed* (which in Greek is *Christos*) to do is proclaim the in-breaking of the kingdom of God, which is seen when justice and mercy reign in our world. Those who are bound by the shackles of injustice, discrimination, marginalization, oppression, fear, and violence are captives that are set free, prisoners that are granted release by God's love and mercy. Conversely, those who are blinded by the greed, selfishness, lust for power, desire for wealth, obsession with control, are granted new sight so that they can see the world as it really is, which means to see the world as God sees it and to change one's life so as to live as a true follower of Christ.

Those who have a vested interest in maintaining the status quo, who are concerned about preserving their own power and control, are likely to find Jesus's proclamation of his mission threatening. It does not take much imagination to see how such a worldview could get someone crucified, for speaking out for and working on behalf of the oppressed necessarily draws undesired attention to the oppressors. To speak the words of justice, mercy, and peace is a powerful statement about how we are to live in the world.

These three first words of Christ reveal to us much about what it means to be Christian and helps to place what happens on the cross on Good Friday within a broader context. When we fixate on the end without taking into account the beginning, we take the words of the Lord out of context. Just as these first words from Luke's account of the Gospel present us with profound insights about our intimacy with God, the centrality of Scripture in forming our identity, and that the way of Christian living is to work for social justice, the Seven Last Words from the cross reiterate the beginning of the Lord's ministry.

These first words, like those that come from the cross, reflect the two sides of *passion*: love and suffering. To have an intimate relationship with God, to make the narrative of Scripture our own story, and to work for social justice in our world requires the surrender of control necessary for love and means that our loving vulnerability and openness will, at times, lead to suffering.

Our love and suffering as Christian disciples, like the Lord's on the cross, does not happen in vain. As the Franciscan scholar Zachary Hayes stated so clearly, "We become like what we love," and that transformation recasts the categories of our ordinary experience into something else, something greater, something more than what we had originally expected. This is not to deny the real pain, loss, and trauma that can accompany suffering and our involuntary loss of control, but it does suggest that the meaning of human experience is deeper and more significant than we generally think (or that our popular culture would have us think).

This is what is at the heart of reflecting on the Seven Last Words of Christ. This, too, is what considering the first words of Christ means for us. Beneath the surface of a few sentences stand profound truths that are not merely historical snippets for us to admire millennia later in our annual recounting of that Good Friday afternoon. Instead, there is a richness to God's revelation, to the divine self-disclosure that takes place in the words passed on to us from the mouth of the Word-made-flesh.

Like Francis of Assisi, we too can be transformed by the power of love and embrace the call to Christian discipleship with *passion*. The task at hand is to see that the Word continues to call us to move beyond ourselves, to enter into an evermore intimate relationship with God, to make God's story our story, to work for justice and peace in our world, and to embrace the love and suffering that comes with following Christ.

1. Timothy Radcliffe, *Seven Last Words* (London: Burns & Oates, 2004), p. 4.

2. Radcliffe, *Seven Last Words*, pp. 5–6.

3. Samuel Taylor Coleridge, *The Complete Poems*, ed. William Keach (New York: Penguin, 1997), p. 275.

4. "Passion" in *Chambers Dictionary of Etymology*, ed. Robert Barnhart (New York: H.W. Wilson, 1988), p. 761.

5. Susan Pitchford, *God in the Dark: Suffering and Desire in the Spiritual Life* (Collegeville, Minn.: Liturgical, 2011).

6. Dialogue from the film *Love Actually*, written and directed by Richard Curtis (Universal Studios Entertainment, 2003).

7. Richard Rohr, *The Naked Now: Learning to See as the Mystics See* (New York: Crossroad, 2009), pp. 123–124.

8. Rohr, *The Naked Now*, p. 123.

9. Rohr, *The Naked Now*, p. 123.

10. Thomas Merton, *Love and Living*, eds. Naomi Burton Stone and Patrick Hart (New York: Harcourt Brace, 1979), pp. 30–31.

11. Merton, *Love and Living*, p. 34.

12. Stanley Hauerwas, *Cross-Shattered Christ: Meditations on the Seven Last Words* (Grand Rapids: Brazos, 2004), p. 15.

13. Damien Vorreux, *First Encounter with Francis of Assisi*, ed. Jean-François Godet-Calogeras (St. Bonaventure, N.Y.: Franciscan Institute, 2012), p. 54.

14. Vorreux, *First Encounter with Francis of Assisi*, p. 54.

15. Zachary Hayes, *Bonaventure: Mystical Writings* (Phoenix: Tau, 1999), pp. 117–118.

16. Vorreux, *First Encounter with Francis of Assisi*, p. 28. For more on the San Damiano cross and the Franciscan tradition, see Michael Guinan, *The Franciscan Vision and the Gospel of John: The San Damiano Cross, Francis and John, Creation and John*, The Franciscan Heritage Series vol. 4 (St. Bonaventure, N.Y.: Franciscan Institute, 2006); and, for a more personal and reflective take, see Susan Saint Sing, *Francis and the San Damiano Cross: Meditations on Spiritual Transformation* (Cincinnati: St. Anthony Messenger Press, 2006).

17. Hayes, *Bonaventure: Mystical Writings*, p. 118.

18. Hayes, *Bonaventure: Mystical Writings*, p. 118.

19. A recent scholarly collection of essays traces the history of Francis's stigmata in the early sources and art. See Jacques Dalarun, Machel Cusato, and Carla Salvati, *The Stigmata of Francis of Assisi: New Studies, New Perspectives* (St. Bonaventure, N.Y.: Franciscan Institute, 2006). Also see Solanus Benfatti, *The Five Wounds of Saint Francis* (Charlotte, N.C.: Tan, 2011).

20. "Dozens Ignored Dying Man on a Sidewalk in Queens," *The New York Times*, April 25, 2010, p. A22.

21. Francis of Assisi, "The Testament," 1–3, in *FAED* 1:124.

22. Thomas of Celano, *The Remembrance of the Desire of a Soul*, V:9, in *FAED* 2:248.

23. Francis of Assisi, "The Earlier Rule," 23:9, in *FAED* 1:85.

24. Radcliffe, *Seven Last Words*, p. 33.

25. Elizabeth Johnson, *Truly Our Sister: A Theology of Mary in the Communion of Saints* (New York: Continuum, 2003), pp. 294–295.

26. Francis Moloney, *The Gospel of John*, Sacra Pagina vol. 4, ed. Daniel Harrington (Collegeville, Minn.: Liturgical, 1998), p. 504.

27. Francis of Assisi, "Admonition VI," 1–3, in *FAED* 1:131.

28. Elizabeth Johnson, *Friends of God and Prophets: A Feminist Theological Reading of the Communion of Saints* (New York: Continuum, 1998), p. 7.

29. Ilia Delio, *Franciscan Prayer* (Cincinnati: St. Anthony Messenger Press, 2004), p. 103.

30. In Greek: Αρχη του ευαγγελιου Ιησου υιου θεου.

31. Alternative English translations of Exodus 3:14 read: "I am who I am," "I am what I am," "I will be what I will be," in addition to others.

32. Leonardo Boff, *Way of the Cross—Way of Justice*, trans. John Drury (Maryknoll, N.Y.: Orbis, 1980), pp. 100–101.

33. The Sacred Exchange, 10, in *FAED*.

34. Radcliffe, *Seven Last Words*, p. 53.

35. William Finnegan, "Leasing the Rain," *The New Yorker*, April 8, 2002.

36. For more on the Franciscan concept of *Transitus* see Daria Mitchell, ed., *Dying, As a Franciscan: Approaching Our Transitus to Eternal Life, Accompanying Others on the Way to Theirs* (St. Bonaventure, N.Y.: Franciscan Institute, 2011).

37. Moloney, *The Gospel of John*, p. 504.

38. Thomas of Celano, *The Life of Saint Francis*, VI:103, in *FAED* 1:273.

39. Thomas of Celano, *The Life of Saint Francis*, Book II, VIII:110, in *FAED* 1:278.

40. Francis of Assisi, "A Letter to the Entire Order," 27–29, in *FAED* 1:118.

About the Author

Daniel P. Horan, O.F.M., is a Franciscan friar of Holy Name Province, a columnist at *America* magazine, and the author of several books including *Dating God: Live and Love in the Way of St. Francis*. He has taught at Siena College and St. Bonaventure University, and has published numerous articles on Franciscan theology and spirituality, Thomas Merton, and contemporary systematic theology. He has lectured around the United States and Europe, currently serves on the board of directors of the International Thomas Merton Society, and is working on a PH.D. in systematic theology at Boston College.